Windham Connecticut

Probate District Records

Volume 1
(1719-1734)

Abstracted by
George Waller

HERITAGE BOOKS
2006

HERITAGE BOOKS
AN IMPRINT OF HERITAGE BOOKS, INC.

Books, CDs, and more—Worldwide

For our listing of thousands of titles see our website
at
www.HeritageBooks.com

Published 2006 by
HERITAGE BOOKS, INC.
Publishing Division
65 East Main Street
Westminster, Maryland 21157-5026

Copyright © 2005 George Waller

All rights reserved. No part of this book may be reproduced or transmitted in any form or by any means, electronic or mechanical, including photocopying, recording or by any information storage and retrieval system without written permission from the author, except for the inclusion of brief quotations in a review.

International Standard Book Number: 978-0-7884-3328-8

Introduction

Probate records are invaluable for genealogists, as these records provide names, dates, places and relationships that form the basis of genealogy. The records are also the product of a legal process concerning important financial matters, and thus are more reliable than, for example, census records.

The Windham Probate District was one of the four original districts formed by act of the General Assembly of October 1719:

"Be it enacted by the Governour, Council and Representatives, in General Court assembled, and by the authority of the same, That there shall be a Court of Probate held at Windham, for the towns of Windham, Lebanon, Coventry, Mansfield, Canterbury, Plainfield, Killingly, Pomfrett, and Ashford, to be held by one judge and clerk, with powers and privileges as the other courts of probate have in this Colony; and in such cases where the law allows liberty of appeal, appeals shall be made to the superiour court in the county of Hartford, where matters in controversy shall happen to be in the county of Hartford; and likewise, where the matter in controversy shall be in the County of New London, appeals shall be made to the superiour court in New London."

With the exception of Woodstock, Massachusetts (now Connecticut), which jutted into the Connecticut colony, this probate district represented the northeastern corner of the current state. During the 1719-1734 period, no towns were added to or deleted from the district.

This book is an abstract of the first volume of the original bound court records preserved in the Windham Probate District Court in the Windham Town Hall, Willimantic, Connecticut. Volume 1 is comprised of two sections covering the years 1719-1734. Section 1 is paged 1-491 and consists of the full range of standard probate court activities: the overseeing and recording of wills, inventories, etc. Section 2 is paged 1-244 and consists primarily of matters concerning guardianships and requests to enter wills, etc. Entries are not always chronological since the clerks would use blank space on pages to fill in short entries from a later date.

As an abstract, this book gives every significant court action. Punctuation, capitalization, and spelling have been modernized except when directly quoted. The names of the judge and clerk have been omitted as excessively repetitive. Interesting items from inventories are mentioned. Real estate is rarely mentioned unless the individual is landless. Editorial comment has been entered between square brackets [ ] and page numbers are also bracketed.

The names and dates of all whose wills or inventories appear here have been compared with the Barbour Collection of Vital Records to add more information to this abstract.

Acknowledgment is given to the Windham Court of Probate and especially Pam Shorey, clerk of the court for her assistance.

This book is to be dedicated to my mother, Jane W. Waller who inspired me to study family history and to my children: Lisa Shea, Jennifer Mottram, Cassion Waller, and Tammy Waller.

Windham (Conn.) Probate Records, Vol 1, Sect.1 (1719-1734)

[1-2] 29 Oct 1719 inv. of estate of George Lillie of Windham, decd taken by Samuel Webb, Samuel Palmer. Includes: books. Total: £455.00.0
[Windham VR 1:18 George Lillie d. 10 Oct 1719]

[3] 12 May 1728 support petition to court by Elsabath Park relict to Isaac Park of Plainfield, decd. Granted.
[Plainfield VR: no record of Isaac Park death]

[4-5] 10 Jun 1719 will of John Huchison Senr of Lebanon "sick & weak in body." To wife Hannah... "her children" ... "my children." To son John Junr. To heirs of my son Jonathan, decd, viz. Hannah Huchison daughter of Jonathan Hutchison. To son Joseph. To son Hezekiah. To son Moses. Execs: wife Hannah and son John. wit: Thomas Root, William Clark. testator: John "X" Huchison.
[Lebanon VR 1:145 John Hutchinson d 21 Dec 1719]

[6-7] 14 Jan 1719/20 inv. of estate of John Huchison of Lebanon, decd, taken by John Gillit, Nathaniel Gove. Total: £638.2.6

[7] [no date] addition to estate of John Hutchison: piece of land in Northampton [Mass]

[8-9] 2 Feb 1713/14 will of Eliezer Brown of Canterbury "stricken in years and attended with infirmaties and many times sickness." Wife Rebecca Brown -- her marriage contract dated 26 Apr 1710 to be faithfully performed by my exec. Son Eliezur, second son Thomas; daus Dinah Davis, Bridgett Fitch; son Deliverance is sole exec.
Wit: Elisha Paine, John Pike. Testator signs Eliezer Brown.
[Canterbury VR 1:95 Dea. Eleazer Brown d 22 Jan 1719/20.]

Windham (Conn.) Probate Records, Vol 1, Sect.1 (1719-1734)

[12-13] 18 Feb 1719/20 inv. of William Douglas of Plainfield, decd who died 22 Jan 1719/20 taken by John Fellows, Ebenezer Harris, John Crery. Includes: Bible, misc. books. Total: £81.1.11
[Plainfield VR 1:18 William Douglas Jr d. 13 Sep 1719.

[13] 11 Aug 1722 court allows to John Dean, adm. to William Douglas of Plainfield, decd for charges as adm. £39.15 and for charges as guardian of Mary Douglas £6.1

[14-15] [4 Jun 1720] inv. of Mr Joseph Blackman of Lebanon, decd taken by William Wattles, Simon Newcombe, John Woodward. Includes two Bibles and other books. Total: £1297.9
[Lebanon VR 1:18 Joseph Blackman d. 20 May 1720.

[16] 29 Jun 1720 will of Thomas Kingsbury of Plainfield, husbandman "sick and weak of body." To wife Sarah sole executrix. To cousin Thomas Kingsbury, my brother Thomas [sic see below] Kingsbury's son of Haverill, Mass. To cousin Bartholomew Kingsbury who lives with me now
land, but if he does not live with his aunt, my wife, until the age of 21, the land goes to Samuel Kingsbury mentioned above.
Wit: Jacob Warren, Joshua Kibbe, Isaac Spaulding
Testator marks with a "T"
[Plainfield VR 1:22 Thomas Kingsbury d. 11 Jun 1720]

[17] 2 Aug 1720 inv. of Thomas Kingsbury taken by Thomas Williams, Jacob Warren, Willliam Dean. Includes books. Total: £190.19.6

[18-20] 10 Dec 1720 will of Joseph Parkhurst of Plainfield, husbandman, "being sick and very weak." To wife Eunice. To sons Timothy, John, Joseph, Samuel. to daus Eunice

2

Windham (Conn.) Probate Records, Vol 1, Sect.1 (1719-1734)

Marsh, Hannah Parkhurst, Mary Parkhurst. Executors: wife Eunice and son John.
Wit: Joseph Warren, William Blodgett, Samuel Spaulding
Testator marks with "P"
[Plainfield VR 1:23 Joseph Parkhurst d. 11 Dec 1720 in the 57th yr of his age]

[20-21] 26 Dec 1720 inv. of Joseph Parkhurst who died 11 Dec 1720 taken by Jacob Warren, Ephraim Kingsbury, Ephraim Wheeler. Includes: Bible and books, land (including 50A in Killingly). [Est. total: £473]

[22] 20 Feb 1720/1 Inheritance to Timothy Parkhurst as gdn to Samuel Parkhurst paid by execs. Wit: Ephraim Wheeler, John How.

[22] 6 Feb 1720/1 each child [of Joseph Parkhurst, decd] gives Samuel Parkhurst £2.0.10 signed Timothy Parkhurst, John Parkhurst, Joseph Parkhurst, Hannah Parkhurst, Thomas Marsh.

[23] 20 Feb 1720/1 set out to Hannah Parkhurst of Plainfield, her portion by execs. Wit: Ephraim Wheeler, John How.

[23] 6 Feb 1720/1 son Samuel Parkhurst paid by Eunice Parkhurst [exec] No witnesses.

[23] 20 Feb 1720/1 Eunice Parkhurst and John Parkhurst, execs pay Timothy Parkhurst and Samuel Parkhurst. Wit: Ephraim Wheeler, John How.

[24] 6 Feb 1720/1 Eunice Parkhurst, exec pays son Joseph. No witnesses.

Windham (Conn.) Probate Records, Vol 1, Sect.1 (1719-1734)

[24] 20 Feb 1720/1 The following ack receipt for their portion: Timothy Parkhurst as guardian to Samuel Parkhurst; Joseph Parkhurst; Timothy Parkhurst; Hannah Parkhurst.

[24] 23 Aug 1722 Mary Parkhurst ack receipt.

[24] 26 Nov 1722 John Parkhurst ack receipt.

[25] 30 Dec 1720 inv. of Joseph Wilson of Ashford who died 24 Dec 1720 taken by Isaac Kendall, Joshua Kendall. Includes books. Total: £180.10.3
[Ashford VR: no death record]

[25] 5 Dec 1722 court allows John Parkhurst expenses for settling estate.

[26] 1 Jun 1721 inv. of Benjamin Smalley of Lebanon, decd taken by Henry Woodward, Josiah Lyman both of Lebanon. Includes: carpenter and joining tools; books and Bibles. Total: £414.0.0
[Lebanon VR: no death record]

[27] 7 Jun 1721 inv. of George Webster decd taken by Joseph Marsh, Samuel Huchison. Includes: land. Total: £1096.9.9

[29-30] 9 Jan 1722[/3] inv. of Lt. Joseph Cary of Windham decd taken by Jonathan Crane, Ralph Wheelock. Includes: sword, shoemaker tools. Total: £361.19.0
[Windham VR A:11 Lt Joseph Cary d. 29 Jun 1722]

[31] 12 Apr 1722 inv. of Joseph Cary Jr decd taken by Nathan Bushnell, Samuel Bingham. Includes: looking glass, two Bibles and books. Total: £222.2.0
[Windham VR 1:54 Lt Joseph Cary d. 10 Jan 1721/2]

Windham (Conn.) Probate Records, Vol 1, Sect.1 (1719-1734)

[31] [undated] inv. of William Shaw decd taken at Windham by Edward Coburn, Robert Molton. Total: 67.18.0

[33] 31 Jan 1715 will of William Shaw of Windham "weak in body." To wife Joannah. To son William [a minor] provided he pay £5 to other children as they reach maturity.
Wit: Robert Moulton, Edward Coburn, Hannah Coburn.
Testator does not sign or mark.
[Windham VR 1:34 William Shaw d. 13 Mar 1715]

[34] 11 Feb 1722/3 inv. of Doctor Isaac Hill of or near Pomfret taken by Smith Johnson, Eleazer Bateman, Jacob Wright. Includes: looking glass, books, sundry goods in Woburn [Mass]. Total: £386.2.3 Addition: goods in the hands of the widow in Woburn inv. taken by Samuel Kendall, Jacob Wright, John Fowle.
[Pomfret VR: no death record]

[35-36] 18 Feb 1722/3 inv. of Capt. Thomas Williams of Plainfield who died 3 Feb 1722/3 taken by Jacob Warren, Joshua Whitney, Timothy Pierce. Includes: armor and cane; Bible and books, looking glass, gun barrel and lock, land in Voluntown. Total: [estimated £1130]
[Plainfield VR 1:27 Capt Thomas Williams d. 3 Feb 1722/3, in the 58th y. of his age]

[37-38] 5 Mar 1722/3 heirs of Thomas Williams agree to split land. Sarah [her mark] Williams, Thomas Williams, Joseph Williams, Ebenezer Williams, Isaiah Williams, Sarah Williams, John Hall gdn to Elizabeth Williams. Wit: Jacob Simon, Nathaniel Webb.

[39] 1 Mar 1722/3 will of William Price of Ashford "weak of body." Son William; daus Sarah and <u>Grace</u>; wife is_ sole exec.

Windham (Conn.) Probate Records, Vol 1, Sect.1 (1719-1734)

Wit: John Barnett, Philip Eastman, Nathaniel Abbot. Testator: no signature.
[Ashford VR A:9 William Price Sr d. 25 Mar 1722/3]

[40-41] 25 Feb 1722/3 will of John Waldin of Windham, yeoman "ill and weak of body" To wife Dorcas as stated in indenture dated 20 Feb 1717/8 between myself and my son John. Son Joseph, Son John only exec. Son Nathaniel. Daughters Mary Waldin and Sarah Waldin. Daus Tabitha Upton, Naomi Dupe, Tamzen Chaplin. Wit: John Lazell, Jonathan Huntington, Eleazer Cary. Testator signs.
[Windham VR: no death date for John. Dorcas Walden, mother of Joseph, d 9 Apr 1748 in the 88th yr of her age.]

[41] 1 May 1723 inv. of John Waldin taken by Eleazer Cary, Richard Abbe. Includes: no land. [Total est £60]

[41] 8 May 1730 Isaac Cary Jr ack rcpt of his part of the estate of his grandmother Mrs. Mary How, decd.

[42] 5 Apr 1723 inv. of William Price of Ashford decd taken by Phillip Eastman, Nathaniel Abbot. Includes: no land. [Total: est £38]

[42-43] 19 Mar 1722/3 will of Nathaniel Skiff, yeoman, "weak of body." To wife Ruth. To son Nathaniel (sole exec). Eldest dau Sarah, dau Abigail, dau Hannah. Wit: Thomas Hartshorn, Daniel Royse, Eleazer Cary. Testator does not sign or mark.
[Windham VR 1:29 Nathaniell Skiff d. 24 Apr 1723 ae. 78]

[43-44] 24 Apr 1723 inv. of Deacon Nathaniel Skiff of Windham, decd taken by Joseph Hibbard, Ralph Wheelock. Includes: Bible and books. Total: £135.19.2

Windham (Conn.) Probate Records, Vol 1, Sect.1 (1719-1734)

[45-46] 19 Sep 1723 inv. of John Ensworth of Canterbury, decd taken by Samuel Butt, Joseph Adams, John Dyer. Includes: books. [Total est: £710]
[Canterbury VR 1:137 John Ensworth d. 25 Aug 1723]

[46] 25/26 Nov 1723 inv. of Mr William Ballard decd taken at Plainfield by Ebenezer Harris, Phillip Bump Jr, John Crery. Includes: books. Total: £430.17.06
[Plainfield VR: no death record]

[47-48] 21 Jul 1721 will of William Ballard of Plainfield, husbandman "sick and weak of body." To wife Hannah. To sons Enoch, Peleg, and Thomas. To dau Hepsobeth [sic]. To kinswoman Sarah Hule. Wife and three sons are execs. Wit: Joseph Coit, John Fellows, Ebenezer Harris. Testator marks.

[49] 15 Jan 1723/4 presented in Windham inv. of Simon Orne of Providence RI decd taken by Joseph Trumbull, John Johnson. Includes: land in Windham. Total: £74

[49] 29 Apr 1724 inv. of Mrs Elizabeth Harris of New London decd. Includes: 100A in Mansfield presented by Mr Samuel Harris, admin. Total: £70

[50] 28 Jul 1724 inv. of Seth Smith of Coventry who died Jun 1724 taken by Francis West, Peter Bewell. Includes: two Bibles and books, a gun. Total: £122.11.00

[51] 7 May 1724 inv. of Benjamin Levins of Killingly who died 7 Apr 1724 taken by Eliezer Bateman, Benjamin Bixby. Includes books. Total: £325.14.06
[Killingly VR no death record]

[51] 25 Sep 1724 above inv. based on what was shown them by his widow Elizabeth Levins.

Windham (Conn.) Probate Records, Vol 1, Sect.1 (1719-1734)

[52] 20-24 Nov 1724 inv. of Lt John Hall decd taken in Plainfield by Ephraim Kingsbury, Ephraim Wheeler, John Crery. Includes: sword and belt, wig, Bible and books, cane, gun, "the negro man servant" £70. [Est. total: £1186]
[Plainfield VR: no death record]

[54] 14 Apr 1724 Lebanon, reappraise land of George Webster by John "B" Bliss, John Webster, Jedidiah Strong.
[Lebanon VR 1:336 George Webster d. 12 Apr 1721]

[55-56] 29 Nov 1724 inv. of Samuel Shepard of Plainfield taken by Ephraim Kingsbury, Daniel Lawrence, Joseph Williams. Includes: new Bible, old Bible, books, a still, a ferry boat, land in Canterbury. [Est. total: £1032]
[Plainfield VR: no death record]

[57] 3 Nov 1724 inv. of Jonathan Davis of Canterbury decd taken by Capt Joseph Adams, Stephen Frost, John Felch. Total: £328.06
[Canterbury VR: no death record]

[57] 14 Jan 1724/5 inv. of Thomas Durkee, husbandman taken at Windham by Thomas Marsh, Nathaniel Kingsbury, Nathaniel Woodward. Includes: books. Total: £135.14.11
[Windham VR: 1:73 Thomas, son of John and Elizabeth Durkee d. 26 Dec 1724]]

[58] 30 Oct 1724 will of Samuel How of Plainfield, carpenter, "very weak and in a decaying condition in my body." Wife Mary; sons Samuel and John (sole exec); to six daughters and Isaac Corey's children each receive 1/7.
Wit: Jacob Warren, Timothy Parkhurst, Samuel Spaulding. The testator signs.
[Plainfield VR 1:34 Samuel How d. 29 Dec 1724]

Windham (Conn.) Probate Records, Vol 1, Sect.1 (1719-1734)

[58] 11 Jan 1724/5 Deacon Jacob Warren, Samuel Spaulding, Timothy Parkhurst attest to oath as witnesses to Samuel How's signature.

[59] 11 Jan 1724/5 inv. of Samuel How of Plainfield who died 30 Dec 1724 taken by Jacob Warren, Ephraim Wheeler, Samuel Spaulding. Includes: Bible and books. [Est. total: £9]

[59] 3 Feb 1724/5 Mr John How makes addition to inv.

[60] Jan 17?? inv. of Jeremiah Durke [of Windham] taken by Thomas Marsh, Nathaniel Kingsbury, Nathaniel Woodward. Includes: looking glass, carpenter's tools, half a sawmill. Total £193.11.05
[Windham VR: 1:73 Jeremiah Durkee son of John and Elizabeth d. 5 Jan 1724/5]

[60] 11 Jan 1725/6 addition to inv. by appraisers.

[61] 3 Jan 1724/5 will of Jeremiah Durke of Windham, housewright "being very sick and weak in body." Everything to wife Elizabeth and she is to pay £10 toward finishing the meeting house. If she remarries then all goes to my brothers and sisters except £70. Exec: "trusty friend" Daniel Holt. Wit: Thomas Marsh, Nathaniel Kingsbury, Nathaniel Woodward. Testator signs.

[61] 22 Jan 1724/5 witnesses affirm signature to above.

[62] 25 Jan 1724/5 inv. of Thomas Whiting of Killingly decd, husbandman, taken by Benjamin Bixby, Jonathan Clough. Total: £109.06.03
[Killingly VR: no death record]

Windham (Conn.) Probate Records, Vol 1, Sect.1 (1719-1734)

[63]   14 Jun 1723 at Windham, John Doget of Attleborough, Mass. and his wife Sarah ack receipt of their share of our father Nathaniel Skiff of Windham decd from brother Nathaniel Skiff. Wit: Anne Ripley, Joshua Ripley. Sarah "Y" Dogget marks.

[63]   13 Jun 1723 at Windham, Hannah Mayhew, relict of Benjamin Mayhew of Chilmark, Mass. decd ack receipt in estate of her father Nathaniel Skiff from her brother Nathaniel. She marks. Wit: John Fitch, Isaac Morgan.

[63]   13 June 1723 at Windham, Isaac Morgan of Preston and Abigail his wife ack receipt in father Nathaniel Skiff's estate from brother Nathaniel Skiff. Wit: John Fitch, Hannah "X" Mayhew. Isaac signs and Abigail marks.

[64]   9 Mar 1724/5   distribution agreement on estate of Mr John Hall of Plainfield, decd. John Smith, Edward Spaulding, Thomas Stevens Jr get a portion. Thomas Stevens Jr, Samuel Hall, Stephen Hall, and the heirs of Thomas Stevens Secundus get a portion. Signed by: John Smith, John Smith atty for Stephen Hall, Edward Spaulding Jr, Thomas Stevens guardian, Thomas Stevens Jr, Thomas Stevens Jr [atty for William Blodgett], Samuel Hall atty for his father. Wit: Elisha Blackman, Joseph Trumbull Jr.

[65]   10 Mar 1724/5 distribution agreement on movables from estate of Mr John Hall of Plainfield decd. £35 each. Sign: John Smith, John Smith atty for Steven Hall, Thomas Stevens guardian, Edward Spaulding Jr, Thomas Stevens Jr, Thomas Stevens Jr atty for William Bloggett, Samuel Hall atty for his father. Wit: Mary "M" Clark, Mindwell "+" Root.

[66]   15 Sep 1730   addition to estate of Lt John Sprague of Lebanon decd by Lois Sprague his exec. She signs.

Windham (Conn.) Probate Records, Vol 1, Sect.1 (1719-1734)

[Lebanon VR 1:280 Lt John Sprague d. 6 Mar 1727/8.]

[66] 8 May 1728 Ephraim Sprague (who signs) ack receipt from his mother Lois Sprague.

[67] 18 Jan 1724/5 inv. of William Hamblett of Pomfret who died 8 Dec 1724. Nathaniel Sessions, Nathaniel Johnson, Leicester Grosvenor chosen by the widow [to take the inventory] and sworn before Col. Chandler of Woodstock. Includes: gun. Total: £734.11
[Pomfret VR:1:32 Wm Hamblett d. 8 Dec 1724]

[68-69] 14 Feb 1724/5 Will of John Adams of Canterbury, yeoman, "very sick and weak in body." Wife Chael[?], exec. Dau Mary; eldest son Samuel; three sons that now live with me, viz John Adams, Isaac Adams, Richard Adams; cousin Ruth Adams (under 18 and living with my wife), dau of Joseph Adams; dau Ruth Pain; youngest son Michael. Exec: wife and son Richard.
Wit: Thomas Brown [?], Timothy Backus, Deliverance Brown. Testator marks "O"
[Canterbury VR:1:66 John Adams d. 16 Feb 1724/5]

[70-72] 18 May 1724/5 inv. of John Adams of Canterbury, decd taken by Deliverance Brown, Timothy Backus, Thomas Brown.. Includes: 1/3 part of a sawmill, sword, bayonet, great gun bullet, Bible, books, two old pieces of Bibles. Total: £352.02.07

[73] 1 Jan 1723/4 Ebenezer Fitch and Bridget Fitch of Windsor (Bridget is dau of Deacon Eliezur Brown of Canterbury, decd) ack receipt from our brother Deliverance Brown of said Canterbury (and son and exec).
Wit: Ebenezer Davis, Mary "X" Tayler. The Fitches sign.

Windham (Conn.) Probate Records, Vol 1, Sect.1 (1719-1734)

[Canterbury VR:1:95: Deacon Eliezur Brown d. 22 Jan 1719/20.

[73] 9 Apr 1720 Thomas Brown of Canterbury, second son of Deacon Eliezer Brown of Canterbury, decd ack receipt from brother Deliverance Brown. Wit: Nathaniel Robbins, Sary "SP" Backus. Thomas Brown signs.

[74] 5 Apr 1720 Eliezer Brown of Concord [Mass], eldest son of Deacon Eliezer Brown of Canterbury, decd ack receipt from brother Deliverance Brown. Wit: Elisha Pain, Elisha Pain Jr. Eliezer Brown signs.

[74] 13 Nov 1722 Ebenezer Davis of Concord [Mass] and Dinah his wife ack receipt from brother Deliverance Brown. Wit: Eliezer Brown, Eliezer Brown Jr. Davises sign.

[75-76] Feb 1724/5 inv. of Phillip Bump of of Canterbury, decd taken by Joshua Whitne, John Fellows, John Crery. Includes: books, looking glass, gun. Total: £266.03.05.
Canterbury VR: no death record]

[76] Dec 1727 addition to the estate of Isaac Parker of Plainfield, decd by Jonathan Dean, John Douglas.
[Plainfield VR: no death record]

[76] 25 Sep 1727 John Burnap of Bath in "Carrolina" son of John Burnap of Windham decd ack receipt of his part of the estate from Isaac Burnap exec. Wit: Dorkas "O" Waldin, Jacob Burnap. John Burnap signs.
[Windham VR: no death record]

[77-78] [undated] inv. of Samuel Sprague of Lebanon who died 21 May 1725 taken by Ephraim Sprague, Henry

12

Windham (Conn.) Probate Records, Vol 1, Sect.1 (1719-1734)

Woodward. Inlcudes: wine glass, looking glass, books. Total: £576.00.00.
[Lebanon VR: no death record]

[78] 28 Jul 1729 an addition to the above made by Ephraim Sprague admin.

[79-80] [undated] inv. of Jonathan Royce of Lebanon who died Apr 1725 taken by John Huchison, Ephraim Sprague. Includes: 2 Bibles, books. Total: £368.00.09
[Lebanon VR:1:260 Jonathan Roice d 10 May 1725]

[81] 17 Jun 1725 inv. of Francis Parker of Canterbury decd taken by Eliezer Batman, Ephraim Warren, Josiah Proctor. Includes: arms and ammunition, books. Total: £273.08.06.
[Canterbury VR: no death record]

[82] 23 Oct 1722 will of James Dean of Plainfield, smith, "grown in years." Wife Sarah; sons James, Willliam, Nathaniel, Jonathan; daus Sarah, Mary, Hannah; grandson Francis Dean. Execs: sons James, John, William. Wit: John Fellows, Ebenezer Harris, Rachel "X" Harris.
[Plainfield VR:1:34 James Dean d. 29 May 1725]

[83] 30 Jun 1725 Plainfield, witnesses affirm signature

[83] 30 Jun 1725 inv. of James Dean of Plainfield, decd who died 29 May 1725. Includes great Bible. Total: £143.9.

[84] 14 Nov 1724 inv. of David Cutting of Killingly, decd taken by Eleazer Bateman, James Levens. Includes arms & ammunition, book, homestead. Total: £96.14.06.
[Killingly VR:1:7 David Cutting d. Oct 1724]

Windham (Conn.) Probate Records, Vol 1, Sect.1 (1719-1734)

[84-85] [no date] inv. of Lt Samll Spaulding of Canterbury, decd. Includes: cane with ivory head, old gun, new gun. Total: £836.18.4.

[86] 6 May [1725] inv. of John Lovejoy of Plainfield who d. 23 Apr 1725 by Deacon Jacob Warren, Ephraim Kingsbury, John How. Includes: gun with new stock, an old gun, powder horns & ammunition, bible and books. Total: est £440.
[Plainfield VR: no death record]

[87] 29 Jun 1725 [inv.] of Robert Willis, decd, by Nathaniel Kingbury, Nathll Barker. Includes: arms & ammunition; carpenter tools; books; land in Ashford. Total: £137.18.
[Ashford VR: no death record]

[87-88] 12 May 1725 inv. of James Richardson, taylor, of Windham, decd. Includes: books; his taylor's tools; house, barn. Total: £475.18.6.
[Windham VR: no death record]

[88] 23 Jul 1725 Nathanll Kingsbury, Richard Abbe sworn.

[89] 8 Dec 1727 Plainfield. William Dean of Plainfield received of my brother John Dean of Groton one of the executors of the will of my father Mr James Dean. Wit: Timo Pierce, Martha Welch (she marks). 9 Dec 1727 rec. by John Crery, clerk of probate.

[90-91] 31 Mar 1725 will of Ephraim Wheeler of Plainfield, millwright "very weak of body and in a languishing condition." To sons: Ephraim, Benjamin, Thomas, Edward at age 21. To daus Elizabeth Huntington, Olive, Mary at age 18. Son Benjamin, sole executor. Wit: Jacob Warren, Samuel Spaulding, Josiah Spaulding. Testator signs will. 27 Apr 1725: witnesses sworn in court; 13 Jul 1725 will exhibited in

Windham (Conn.) Probate Records, Vol 1, Sect.1 (1719-1734)

court and ordered recorded [note that this is the first time this type of statement is used in the court records]
[Plainfield VR:1:34 Ephraim Wheeler d. 19 Apr 1725]

[91-92]   29-30 Apr 1725 inv. of Ephraim Wheeler, of Plainfield, decd taken by Jacob Warren, Ephraim Kingsbury, John Howe. Includes: gun & sword & belt & girdle; Bible and books. Total real estate: £565, total personal estate £169.13.19. Total: £734.13.9.

[92]   11 May 1725   will of Jonathan Rigby of Plainfield, husbandman, "sick and weak of body." To wife Hannah who is sole exec. To dau Susanna (she is under 18). Wit: Jacob Warren, Benjamin Spaulding, John Hallowell. Testator marks. 13 Jul 1725 witnesses sworn; 13 Jul 1725 will exh. and ord to be recorded.
[Plainfield VR:1:41 Jonathan Wright [sic] d 11 May 1725 in the 26th year of his age]

[93]   3 Jun 1725   inv of Jonathan Rigby, decd taken by Ephraim Kingsbury, Samuel Spaulding and John Howe. Includes: holsters & pistols; shoe maker tools; land in Canterbury. Total: £440.9.6.

[94]   24 Sep 1725   Plainfield. Mr Ephraim Davis, admin of est of Jonathan Davis of Canterbury, decd. Court distributes: to Mary Davis, sister of decd; to Elizabeth Davis, sister of decd; Daniel Davis brother of decd; Hannah Davis, sister of decd. Court orders Capt. Joseph Adams, Mr John Felch of Canterbury, and Mr Joseph Williams of Plainfield to distribute above. Court appts Mr Nathaniel Pond of Canterbury gdn for above Hannah Davis.
[Plainfield VR: no death record]

Windham (Conn.) Probate Records, Vol 1, Sect.1 (1719-1734)

[95] 27 Sep 1725 Plainfield Sarah Hill, exec for Dr Isaac Hill of Pomfret, decd exhibits acct of distribution.

[95] 29 Jun 1728 Matthew Huntington of Norwich ack rcpt from Benjamin Wheeler of Plainfield, exec of his father's will, the portion to his dau Elizabeth Huntington. Wit: Sarah Meriam, Lydia "C" Huntington. MH signs. 12 Nov 1728 recorded.

[95] 12 Nov 1728 Plainfield Thomas Wheeler ack rcpt of est of his father Mr Ephraim Wheeler from Benjamin Wheeler, exec. Wit: Timothy Pierce, John Crery. TW signs.

[96-97] 22 Apr 1725 will of Nathaniel Hobart of Windham "weak and low in body." To wife Sarah, she and my bro Joseph Hobart and Eleazer Cary execs; sons: Nathaniel, eldest; Jonathan, 2nd; Paul, 3rd; Zebulon 4th; Elisha 5th; Gideon, youngest. To daus at marriage: Ann, eldest; Deborah 2nd; Sarah, youngest. Testator signs. Wit: Jonathan Huntington, Robert Hobart, Ebenezer Hobart
[name also spelled Hebard and Hobard]. 29 Jun 1725 Witnesses sworn; 23 Jul 1725 will exh and recorded.
[Windham VR:1:2 Sgt Nathl Hibbard d. 26 Apr 1725]

[97] 4 Dec 1727 Canterbury Edward Spaulding ack recpt from Bemjamin Wheeler, exec of Ephraim Wheeler of Plainfield, decd. £10 for bringing up youngest dau. ES marks. Wit: Elisha Paine, Constance Pain. 12 Nov 1728 recorded.

[98] 4 & 8 Nov 1725 inv of Benjamin Palmer of Plainfield, decd by Nathaniel Juol [i.e. Jewell], Joseph Williams, Thomas Stevens Jr. No real estate. Total: £57.
[Plainfield VR: no death record]

Windham (Conn.) Probate Records, Vol 1, Sect.1 (1719-1734)

[99] 7 Jun 1725 inv of Nathaniel Hebard of Windham, decd by Jonah Palmer, Richard Abbe. Includes: books, his arms; farm £600. Total: L700.09.6. 21 Jun 1725 appraisers take oath.

[100] 25 Sep 1725 inv of Mr John Burnap, of Windham, decd by Samuel Palmer, Richard Abbe. Includes: books, arms. Total: £61.15.8. 1 Oct 1725 appraisers take oath.

[100-101] 11 Sep 1725 inv of Mr Robert Simons, [town not given], decd. Includes: books; wig; old sword; looking glass; gun. Total: £52. 21 Dec 1725 Capt Eliezer Cary, Benjamin Holt take appraisers oath.

[102-103] 13 Sep 1725 inv of Sgt Edward Spaulding of Plainfield, decd by Deac. Jacob Warren, William Marsh, John How. Includes: Bible & books. Total: £280. Signed by JW, WM Jr [!] and JH. 19 Oct 1725 additions to inv. Recorded 14 Feb 1727/8.
[Plainfield VR: no death record]

[103] 12 Feb 1733/4 additions to est of Edward Spaulding by Dorothy ("X") Spaulding.

[103] 9 Feb 1725/6 Mary ("X") Spaulding ack recpt from Dorothy Spaulding from her father [no name given] of Plainfield, decd. 30 Apr 1728 recorded.

[104] 6 Dec 1729 Plainfield Abigail Powell of Plainfield received of my mother Mary Button and my brother Peter Button £1. She signs. Wit: Josiah ("C") Cleveland, Elizabeth (her mark) Cleveland. 1 Jun 1730 recorded.

[105-106] 7 Oct 1725 Canterbury Joseph Adams, John Felch, Joseph Williams by order dated 24 Sep 1725, distribute

Windham (Conn.) Probate Records, Vol 1, Sect.1 (1719-1734)

est of Mr Jonathan Davis of Canterbury, decd to his brothers and sisters being four in number. Split estate in four parts. To brother Daniel, to eldest sister Mary, to 2nd sister Elizabeth, to youngest sister Hannah. Their father Ephraim Davis mentioned. 14 Dec 1725 distr. accepted and recorded.

[106] 7 Oct 1725 Canterbury ack rcpt from father Ephraim Davis... Mary, Elizabeth, Daniel, Hannah Davis sign with Nathaniel Bond guardian.

[107-108] 11 Jul 1725 inv of William Clark Esq. of Lebanon, decd by Jonathan Clark and Joseph Clark. Includes books, wine glass, inkhorn, pair of spectacles, gun, sword, pair of shilyards. Total: £712.18.10.
[Lebanon VR: 1:40 Capt William Clark d. 9 May 1725 in the 69th year of his age.]

[108-110] 9 Dec 1725 William Clark Esq. of Lebanon, decd distribution. Wife Mary; sons William, Jonathan, Joseph, Benoni, Timothy, Gershom, and Ebenezer Hunt for Hannah Hunt his wife and sister of the above; and Thomas Clark of Waterbury. Widow marks, rest sign.

[111-115] Oct & Nov 1725 inv. of Rev. Samuel Whiting of Windham, decd. Includes: Bible & books (50 named, ca 94 unnamed); one old Bible; a large looking glass; six wine glasses. Taken by John Fitch, Richard Abbe. 9 Dec 1725 inventors sworn. Total: £1177.18.1.
[Windham VR:1:54 Rev Saml Whiting d 27 Sep 1725 in Enfield]

[116] 27 Apr 1727 additions by Richard Abbe and Elizabeth Whiting admin, recorded.

Windham (Conn.) Probate Records, Vol 1, Sect.1 (1719-1734)

[117-118] 24 Feb 1725/6 agreement to distr. of estate of Phillip Bump of Plainfield, decd. Samuel Bump of Bolton; Phillip Bump & Josiah Bump of Plainfield; Thomas Smith of Preston for Jemima his wife and a sister; Thomas Hord of Plainfield for Lydia his wife and a sister; Peleg Ballard of Plainfield for Bethia his wife and a sister; Sarah Bump of Plainfield, a sister. Est appraised at £266.3.5. Sarah Bump, widow. Signed Sarah ("O") Bump, Samuel ("backward S") Bump, Phillip Bump, Josiah Bump and Thomas Smith sign; Thomas ("X") Hord; Peleg ("X") Ballard, Sarah ("X") Bump.

[119-120] 6 Mar 1726 [1725/6] Ambros Blunt of Norwich received of Isaac Burnap of Windham his share is his wife's portion of her father John Burnap, of Windham, decd est. Recorded 11 Apr 1726. Jacob Burnap of [not given]; Joseph Smith of Canterbury on behalf of his wife; Joshua Lasell of Windham due to his children from his mother; and Abraham Burnap of Norwich all ackn. rcpt from Isaac Burnap from John Burnap of Windham, decd.

[121] 7 Apr 1726 Martha Barker of Killingly, adm. to husband Francis Barker of Killingly, decd quitclaims all her rights to real estate to Jacob Spaulding and Hannah his wife and to Judith Barker of Concord [MA] and to Dorothy Barker of Killingly. Wit: Ephraim Kingsbury, John How. Martha marks "X" Recorded 23 Apr 1726.
[Killingly VR: no death record]

[122] 12 Apr 1726 Daniel Lawrence and Sarah his wife of Plainfield bound to Thomas Williams of Plainfield who is exec. of Thomas Williams Esq of Plainfield, decd. Wit: John Crery, Ephn Fellows. DL signs, SL marks.
[Plainfield VR:1:27 Capt Thomas Williams d. 3 Feb 1723/4 in the 58th year of his age]

Windham (Conn.) Probate Records, Vol 1, Sect.1 (1719-1734)

[123] 12 Jul 1726 additional est to James Dean.

[123-124] 18 May 1726 inv. of Mr Joseph Woodward of Canterbury, decd. Includes: books. Total: £176.17.2.
[Canterbury VR:1:246 Joseph Woodward d. 14 May 1726]

[124] 13 Sep 1726 Mr John Hutchison adm of Jonathan Rice of Lebanon, decd.
[Lebanon VR:1:269 Jonathan Rice d. 28 Apr 1725]

[124] 13 Sep 1726 Mrs Ruth Rice adm of Jonathan Rice granted support from the estate.

[125] 14 Sep 1726 Edward Spaulding and Elisabeth Spaulding his wife, sister of Lt John Hall of Plainfield, decd. John Smith and Susannah his wife, sister of same. Thomas Stevens Jr is adm. They request distribution. Recorded 15 Sep 1726.

[126] 6 Oct 1726 Mr Jacob Simons adm of the estate of Mr Robert Simons of Windham, decd distributed to Mr Jonathan Simons, Mr David Simons, Mr Jacob Simons, Mr Ebenezer Simons. Court appts Mr Benjamin Scott, Mr Jeremiah Ripley, and Mr Benjamin Follett to [re]distribute the estate. 16 Dec 1726 [orig] distr reversed by misinformation.
[Windham VR:1:10 Robert Simons d. 29 Aug 1724 ae nearly 79 years]

[127-128] 16 Sep 1726 will of Jonathan Hides of Canterbury "very sick." Wife Abigail's marriage contract to be fulfilled;.sons Jonathan Hides and James Hides; six daughters: Dorothy wife of Joseph Parham, Hannah wife of John Woodward, Mary relict of Daniel Carpenter, decd, Elizabeth wife of Isaac Farwell, Sarah wife of John Pike?, Abigail, decd, late wife of Joseph Cleveland. Jonathan Hides appt sole exec.

Windham (Conn.) Probate Records, Vol 1, Sect.1 (1719-1734)

Testator signs. Wit: John Adams, Abigail Brown, Deliverance Brown. 8 Oct 1726 wit oath and will ord recorded.
[Canterbury VR: no death record]

[129] 5 Oct 1726 Canterbury inv of Mr Jonathan Hides of Canterbury, decd by Thomas Brown, Joseph Adams, Deliverance Brown. Includes: old Bible & books; two powder horns; old sword. Total: £186.19.7.

[130-131] 4 May 1726 will of Benjamin Franklin of Pomfret, cooper, "weak in body." All to son-in-law and dau Thomas Bettis. Other ch already received their part. Wit Nathaniel Johnson, Leicester Grosvenor, Henry Bowen. 22 Jun 1726 wit oath; 13 Sep 1726 will proven; 9 Dec 1726 will recorded.
[Pomfret VR:1:29 Benj Franklin Sr d. 4 Jun 1726]

[131-133] 13 Apr 1726 will of John Mory of Lebanon, weaver(?) "being very sick and weak in body."
wife Margaret; eldest son Linsford; 2nd son Ephraim (under 21), youngest son John. Exec: wife and trusty friend Lt Joseph Markain of said Lebanon. Wit: William Gager, Benoni Clark, James Tuttle, Ephraim Lumes. 11 May 1726 wit. oath; 13 Sep 1726 will proven; 10 Jan 1726/7 will recorded.
[Lebanon VR: no death record]

[133] [undated] inv of John Morey, decd taken by Richard English, Henry Glover. Includes: loom, Bible & books, gun. Total: £321.02.3. 6 Feb 1726/7 recorded.

[134] 1 Oct 1719 dist of George Lillie by Samuel Webb, Jonathan Silsby, Samuel Palmer:
Jacob Lillie double portion; Elisha Lillie; Reuben [Lillie]; Elizabeth [no surname given]; Mary [no surname given]; Lidia [no surname given]; Sarah [no surname given]; Bethiah [no

Windham (Conn.) Probate Records, Vol 1, Sect.1 (1719-1734)

surname given]. No relationships stated. 23 Mar 1721 appr oath; 13 Dec 1726 dist ordered recorded.

[135] 19 Mar 1725[/26] Plainfield received of John How, exec of his father Samuel How of Plainfield, decd, £37.16 by widow Mary ("X") How. Wit: David Munroo, James Holkins. [Plainfield VR:1:34 Samuel How d. 29 Dec 1724]

[135] ditto L5.8 left to my wife, Isaac Wheeler marks. Wit: James Holkins, Thomas Wheeler.

[135] ditto left to my wife, David Munroo signs. No witnesses.

[135] ditto left to my wife, John Stevens signs. No wit.

[135] 13 Jun 1726 ditto left by my father Mary ("+") Russell. No wit.

[136] 7 Jun 1726 ditto Mary ("M") Farar.

[136] 19 Mar 1725[/26] ditto left to my wife, John Parkhurst signs. 6 Feb 1726/7 recorded.

[136-137] 23 Sep 1726 inv of James Leech, decd appraised at Windham by Thomas Durkee and Clement Neff of Windham. Mary Leech, admin. Includes: one Bible and "sundry good books;" two old guns with but one lock, an old cutlash; large looking glass. Total: est £70.
[Windham VR:1:60 James Leech d. 12 Sep 1726 aet about 72 years]

[138-139] 27 Nov 1726 Samuel Throop of Lebanon "being very weak and sick in body." To wife Dorothy, to all my children (unnamed), to my father Dan Throop who is also my

exec. Wit: William Throop, Saml Murdock, Joseph Fowler. Testator signs.
[Lebanon VR: no death record]

[139]   16 Dec 1726   Windham   wit oath.   9 Feb 1726/7 recorded.

[139]   8 Sep 1729   addition to est of Mr James Leech by appraisers Clement Neff, Thomas Durkee.

[140]   13 Dec [1726]   inv of Samuel Throop, decd taken by Simon Newcomb, Joseph Phelps. Incl: one Indian man, one Indian woman, one Indian child, one Negro man, 2 wigs, pistols. Total: est £2350.

[141]   1726   inv of James Welch, decd by Deac Joshua Whitney, Phillip Bump, Joseph Lawrence. Incl: Bible, land at Voluntown. Total: est £117.

[142]   1 Feb 1726?/27]   Andrew Alden of Lebanon and Daniel Hyde of Norwich appt to appraise est of Josiah Baker of Lebanon. Includes: inkhorn; note from Caleb Hyde; bond from Samuel Crocker Jr; note from Robert Cathcart; note from Jonathan Bill; note from John West; note from Mr George Partridge; due from Daniel Hyde's est; Samuel Coggwell debtor; Samuel Hyde Jr debtor; Jeremiah Mason debtor, John Fitch of Windham debtor; carpenter and joyner tools. Total: £178.12.9.   10 Feb 1726/7 recorded.
[Lebanon VR: no death record]

[143-147]   21 Nov 1726 distribution of est of Mr Samuel Shepard of Plainfield, decd by Jacob Warren, Ephraim Kingsbury, Daniel Lawrence. To Mrs Eleanor Shepard, relict; to Jonathan Shepard eldest son; to David Shepard 2nd son; to Nathan Shepard 3rd son; to Benjamin Shepard 4th son; to

Windham (Conn.) Probate Records, Vol 1, Sect.1 (1719-1734)

Eleanor Darby wife of James Darby; to Mary Johnson wife to Jacob Johnson land in Canterbury; to Luce(?) Shepard land on Quinebaug River. 7 Dec 1726 distribution exh. and ord. recorded. 14 Feb 1726/27 rec.
[Plainfield VR: no death record]

[147] no date Deacon Joshua Whitney appt gdn to Jonathan and David Shepard; no date Mr David Whitney appt gdn to Nathan and Benjamin Shepard.

[148] 12 Apr 1726 application by Mrs Hannah Rigbee relict to Mr Jonathan Rigbee late of Plainfield for support. Court sets out £50 for support.

[149] 12 Apr 1726 heirs of Mr Samuel Spalding are dissatisfield with the distribution of the woodlot to the widow. Mary Spalding marks, Samuel Spalding marks, Jonas Spalding signs, Mary Spalding signs, John Woodward signs, Joseph Cleveland signs, Zachariah Spalding signs.

[150] 6 Jun 1726 William Whiting of Norwich ack rcpt of my father Samuel Whiting of Windham my portion. Signs. Wit: Thomas Clapp, Mary Whiting. 27 Apr 1727 recorded.

[150] 9 Mar 17[26/]27 Joseph Fitch of Lebanon ack rcpt of father-in-law Rev. Mr Samuel Whiting of Windham, decd the portion belonging to his dau. Ann Fitch. 27 Apr 1727 recorded.

[150] 22 Mar 1727 John Backus Jr ditto for his wife Sybil Backus. 27 Apr 1727 recorded.

[151] page is blank

Windham (Conn.) Probate Records, Vol 1, Sect.1 (1719-1734)

[152-155] 27 Sep 1725 distr. of est of Rev. Mr Samuel Whiting of Windham, decd by John Fitch, Samuel Webb, Jeremiah Ripley. To William Whiting, eldest son; to John Whiting, Eliphalet Whiting, Elisha Whiting, Samuel Whiting, Joseph Whiting, Nathan Whiting, Ann Fitch, Elizabeth Gager, Sybil Backus, Mary Whiting. 29 Apr 1726 distr. exh. and ord. rec. 27 Apr 1727 recorded.

[156] 17 Dec 1726 General Assembly of 13 Oct 1726 ordered part of Rev. Mr Samuel Whiting's estate to be sold.

[156] 11 Jun 1728 an addition to the est of James Welch of Plainfield, decd by James Welch admin.

[157] 3 Apr 1727 Edward Spaulding ack rcpt of his portion of the est of Lt John Hall of Plainfield from Thomas Stevens, admin on behalf of his wife Elizabeth as sister to the decd. Wit: Thomas Rose, Jos. Williams.

[157] 4 Apr 1727 Isaac Shepard ack rcpt of his portion of the est of Lt John Hall of Plainfield from Thomas Stevens, admin on behalf of our mother Ruth Stevens, decd, sister to the decd. Wit: Isaac ("I") Shephard, Jonas Shephard.

[157] 4 Apr 1727 Nathaniel Pierce and Elizabeth Pierce [same as above] Wit: Isaac Shephard (signs).

[158] 30 Mar 1727 Samuel Hall [same as above] he is son of Samuel Hall, brother of the decd. Wit: Jos. Williams, Thomas Rose. 17 May 1727 recorded.

[158] 3 Apr 1727 Thomas Stevens 2nd atty for Thomas Stevens and Zebulon Stevens and guardian to Uriah, Andrew, Benjamin, Samuel and Zebulon Stevens son to Mary Stevens, sister to Lt John Hall etc. ack rcpt. Thomas Stevens, guardian,

signs. Wit: Jos. Williams, Thomas Rose. 17 May 1727 recorded.

[159] 3 Apr 1727 Thomas Stevens Jr atty for William Bloggett and his wife Sarah, sister to Lt. John Hall ack rcpt. Wit: Jos. Williams, Daniel Lawrence. 17 May 1727 recorded.

[159] 4 Apr 1727 Thomas Stevens Jr, John Stevens, _____ Stevens and Ruth ("X") Stevens, children of Ruth Stevens, sister to Lt John Hall. Wit: Eleazer Brown, Jediah Pierce. 17 May 1727 recorded.

[159] 3 Apr 1727 John Smith for my wife Susannah, sister to Lt John Hall, decd. ack rcpt. 17 May 1727 recorded.

[160] 3 Apr 1727 John Smith, atty for Stephen Hall, brother to Lt John Hall. Wit: Jos. Williams, Thomas Rose. 17 May 1727 recorded.

[161] __ Jan 1726/7 inv of Hezekiah Mason appr at Windham by John Fitch, Abraham Mitchell. Incl: powder horn and powder, Bible & books, inkhorn. Tot: est £25. 17 May 1727 recorded.
[Windham VR:1:79 Hezekiah Mason d. 15 Dec 1726]

[162-165] 21 Feb 1726/27 inv of Deac Samuel Stetson appr at Mansfield by Thomas Huntington, Thomas Storrs, Ebenezer Dunham. Incl: Bible & books listed, gun and ammunition, farm £800, mill and tools, canoe. Tot: est £1150. 22 May 1727 recorded.
[Mansfield VR (Dimmock, 342) Deac Samuel Stetson d. 4 Jan 1726/7]

[165-167] 24 Feb 1726/27 inv of Steven Lee of Lebanon, decd taken by Ebenezer Williams, Caleb Huntington.

Windham (Conn.) Probate Records, Vol 1, Sect.1 (1719-1734)

Includes: house/farm £210, looking glass, two old Bibles and books. 24 May 1727 recorded.
[Lebanon VR:1:176 Stephen Lee d. 5 Sep 1725]

[167-170] 9 Jan 1726/27 will of Thomas Cushman of Lebanon "being very sick and weak in body." Wit: Abel Wright Jr, Caleb Pierce, John Woodward.
Son William, son Thomas, son Eleazer, eldest dau Zibiah Cushman, dau Ruth Cushman under 18, dau Lydia under 18. 28 Feb 1726/27 wit oath; 7 May 1727 exh and ordered recorded; 24 May 1727 recorded.
[Lebanon VR: no death recorded]

[170-173] [undated] inv of Thomas Cushman of Lebanon, decd taken by John Woodward, Benjamin Brewster. Incl: house/land £400, looking glass, Bible and other books. Total est £1126.

[174-177] [undated] inv of Josiah Luce of Windham taken by Nathaniel Rudd, Samuel Bingham, Ebenezer Hebard. Incl: one Bible, book, part of two old Bibles, one sword, on old fire lock, one round barrild fire lock, farm 81A £455. Total est. £760. 26 May 1727 recorded. 14 Feb 1737/38 addition to inventory: due from Saml Palmer Jr £2.5.0.
[Windham VR: death not recorded]

[178-181] 4 Apr 1727 distr of est of Lt John Hall, decd by Daniel Lawrence, Thomas Rose, Joseph Williams.
Mr Samuel Hall, eldest bro of decd; Mr Steven Hall, 2nd of Charlestown MA bro of decd; heirs of Ruth Stephens, eldest dau of decd; Mrs Susannah Smith, 2nd dau of decd; Mary Stevens, 3rd dau of decd; Elizaabeth Spaulding, 4th dau of decd; Sarah Bloggett, youngest dau of decd. 5 Apr 1727 distr exh and ord rec; 26 May 1727 recorded.

Windham (Conn.) Probate Records, Vol 1, Sect.1 (1719-1734)

[181] 17 Apr 1727 Olive ("X") Wheeler of Plainfield ack rcpt from her bro Benjamin Wheeler, admin to her father's will. Wit: William Marsh, Isaac Wheeler. 13 Jun 1727 recorded.

[182-183] 13 May 1727 will of Joseph Woodward of Windham "sick and weak in body." Only son Joseph Woodward is to raise siblings; dau Bethia under 21; youngest dau Elizabeth under 21. Brothers John Woodward and Richard Woodward, execs. Testator marks. wit: Jonathan Silsby, Samll Cook, Eleazer Cary. 13 Jun 1727 wit oath, will exh and ordered recorded. 23 Jun 1727 recorded.
[Windham VR:1:84 Joseph Woodward d. 30 May 1727]

[183-185] 1 Jun 1727 inv of Joseph Woodward of Windham, decd tken by Eleazer Cary, Jonath Silsby, Samll Cook. Incl: a gun, old Bible and books (some by title), looking glass, dwelling house £400. Total est £500.

[186] 1 May 1727 inv of Mr Caleb Conant of Windham, decd taken by Jeremiah Bolen, Richard Abbe.
[Windham VR: no death recorded]

[187-188] 18 May 1727 will of Israel Luce of Windham, yeoman. Wife Grace; son Joseph (with whom Grace lives) is exec; son Benjamin under 21; eldest dau Thankful Luce under 18; 2nd dau Mary Luce under 18; youngest dau Ann Luce. Wit: Joshua Wright, Elizabeth Rudd, Eleazer Cary. 26 Jun 1727: wit oath, will exh and ord rec; recorded.
[Windham VR:1:22 Israel Luce d. 20 May 1727]

[188] 28 Feb 1733/34 addition to estate of Mr James Tisdale of Lebanon, decd taken by Nathaniel Fitch, Ebenezer Tisdale execs.
[Lebanon VR:1:1:309 James Tisdale d. 2 May 1727]

Windham (Conn.) Probate Records, Vol 1, Sect.1 (1719-1734)

[189-190] 1 Jun 1727 inv of Israel Luce, decd taken by John Bass, Jonah Palmer. Incl: gun & sword, powder horn. Total est £450.

[190-192] 1 Apr 1727 will of James Tisdale "weak in body." Wife: Mrs Mindwell Tisdale that which she brought with her; dau Sybil, wife of Jonathan Ladd; eldest son Ebenezer; dau Mary Tisdale; dau Margaret Tisdale; son James Tisdale; son William Tisdale; dau Abigail Tisdale; son Solomon Tisdale; Son Antipas Tisdale; dau Phoebe. Sons to receive at 21 and daus at marriage or 21. Wit: Noah Strong, John Sprague, Josiah Wheeler. 30 May 1727 Wit oath in Lebanon; 27 Jun 1727 James Tisdale of Lebanon will exh and ord rec. 19 Jun 1727 recorded.

[192-193] 30 May 1727 inv of Mr James Tisdale, of Lebanon, decd taken by Preserved Strong, Daniel Holbrook, Joseph Phelps. Incl: silver head of a cane, two guns, Bible and books, set of smith tools, no land. Total: £1022.18.3. 17 Aug 1727 recorded.

[194-195] 23 Jun 1727 inv of Samuel Manning Jr taken at Windham by John Spencer and Eleazer Cary. Inlc: pslam book, gun and sword and belt, pound of powder, three pounds of bullets, a compass, looking glass, no land. Tot: est £60. 28 Aug 1727 recorded; ditto addition; 14 Jun 1728 addition recorded.
[Windham VR: no death record]

[196-197] 8 Aug 1727 agreement of only heirs of Francis Barker of Killingly decd to distribute. To Hannah Spaulding, wife of Jacob Spaulding and eldest sister of decd; to Dorothy Wilson, wife of John Wilson and youngest sister of decd; to Judith Barker, 2nd sister of decd. Hannah ("H") Spaulding,

Windham (Conn.) Probate Records, Vol 1, Sect.1 (1719-1734)

Dorothy ("mark") Wilson, Judith ("J") Barker. 8 Aug 1727 ack in court; ditto ordered recorded; 19 Aug 1727 recorded.

[198] 24 Feb 1725/226 agreement: Mary Palmer relict of Mr Benjamin Palmer of Plainfield, decd and Joseph Lawrence of Plainfield regarding real estate. Deacon Joshua Whitney and Mary Whitney (she is sole heir to the decd). Wit: Ephraim Kingsbury, Phelix Powel. 24 Feb 1725/26 ack; 1 Sep 1727 recorded.

[199] 8 Nov 1725 Joshua Whitney of Plainfield and Mary his wife for love and affection give to Joseph Lawrence and Mary his wife our rights in the est of our father and mother Benjamin Palmour and Mary his wife of Plainfield. Joshua signs, Mary marks "M" Wit: Ebenezer Harris, John Crery. Rec 4 Sep 1727.

[200] 12 Sep 1727 inv of Isaac Park of Plainfield, decd taken by Daniel Lawrence, Jonathan Dean. Incl: Bible, powder, six flints. Tot est: £180.

[201-202] 13 Sep 1727 inv of Miles Jordan of Voluntown, decd taken by Jacob Bacon, Rober Park, Nathaniel Dean. Incl: land bought from his son Miles Jordan on "colony presumed line;" three guns. Support of widow and children given. 26 Sep 1727 rec. [no date]: addition made by admin Elizabeth "her mark" Jordan.
[Voluntown VR: no death record]

[203-205] 1 Jul 1725 will of Mathias Button of Plainfield. Wife Mary; son Daniel Button; son Mathias Button, son Peter Button husbandry tools; dau [first name not given] Hill; dau Sarah Marsh (if she dies then to her dau Sarah Marsh); dau Abigail Powell; dau Zerviah Button; son Peter and my wife exec. Wit: Joseph "." Johnson, Sarah "S" Blodgett, Hannah

Windham (Conn.) Probate Records, Vol 1, Sect.1 (1719-1734)

"X" Pierce. 9 Oct 1727 wit oath; 9 Oct 1727 ord rec. 24 Oct 1727 rec.
[Plainfield VR: no death recorded]

[205] 18 Oct 1725 Samuel "X" Howe ack rcpt from John Howe exec of my father Samuel Howe of Plainfield, decd. Wit: James Holkens, Josiah Howe.

[206] 25 Sep 1727 inv of Matthias Button of Plainfield, decd taken by Daniel McMaines, Isaac Cory, James Marsh. Incl: books. Total est: £53. Widow mentioned.

[207-208] inv of Mr John Howe, of Plainfield decd taken by John Crery, Ephraim Kingsbury, Daniel Lawrence. Incl: books, 3 bibles, best gun, another gun, joyner's tools, 1000 cedar clapboards. Mentions support for family. 3 Nov 1727 rec.
[Plainfield VR:1:42 John Howe d. 27 Aug 1727]

[209] 25 Oct 1727 inv of Mary Howe, widow and relict of Samuel Howe late of Plainfield, both decd taken by Ephraim Kingsbury, William Marsh Jr, Samuel Starns Tot est £50.
[Plainfield VR:1:34 Mary Howe d. 1 Sep 1727]

[210] 25 Oct 1727 inv of Mr John Carter decd taken at Canterbury by Benjamin Fassett, John Felch.
[Canterbury VR: no death recorded]

[211] [no date] inv of Robert Miller [town not given] taken by Nathaniel Dean, David Dill. Total est £280. 7 Dec 1727 rec. 10 Apr 1728 addition by Robert Milar, adm.

[212-214] 6 Nov 1727 inv of Mr Tixwell Ensworth decd taken at Canterbury by Samuel Butt, Solomon Tracy, John Felch. Incl: Bible and books, two guns. Tot est £270.

31

Windham (Conn.) Probate Records, Vol 1, Sect.1 (1719-1734)

[Canterbury VR: no death record; name prob. Tyxhall]

[214]   25 Nov 1728   Mrs Elizabeth Jordan adm. of Miles Jordan of Voluntown decd. General Assembly granted her appeal to sell some land. £188.8.5 to be sold.

[215] [undated] inv of Jacob Ardway of Mortlake, decd taken by Abel Wright, Nathaniel Bliss, Nathl Holbrook. Tot est £410. 22 Dec 1729 rec.
[Pomfret/Canterbury VR: no death recorded]

[215-218]   7 Sep 1727 inv of Mr Samuel Storrs, decd, taken at Mansfield by John Arnold, Thomas Storrs, Josiah Conant. Incl 3 Bibles, two house lots in town. Tot est £1700.
[Mansfield VR (Dimmock, 342) Samuel Storrs d. 9 Aug 1727]

[219]   13 Sep 1727 inv of Richard Gayle, decd taken by Samuel Butt, Edward Raynsford, John Dyer. Incl: gun and sword. Tot est: £600.

[220-222]   9 Nov 1727 inv of David Carver of Canterbury taken by Solomon Tracy, John Felch, Joseph Adams. Incl: books, large looking glass, old compass. Tot est: £1800.
[Canterbury VR:1:117 Ens. David Carver d. 14 Sep 1727]

[223-224]   3 Nov 1727 inv of Jonathan Simons of Windham, decd taken by Jonah Parmour, Jacob Simons. Incl: four powder horns, powder, gun, bayonet. Tot. est £600.
[Windham VR:1:10 Jonathan Simons d. 14 Sep 1727 aet. 46 years 5 months]

[224-225]   14 Apr 1727 inv of John Hutchison of Lebanon, decd taken by John "I" Sullivan, John Newcombe. Incl: two guns, a rapier and belt, a cutlass, books. Tot est: £550.

Windham (Conn.) Probate Records, Vol 1, Sect.1 (1719-1734)

[Lebanon VR:1:140 John Hutchison Sr d 9 Feb 1727 in the 43rd year of his age]

[226] 11 Jan 1727/8 distr of est of Mr Isaiah Backer(?) of Lebanon, decd by Josiah Bartlett, Ephraim Kingsbury. To bro Samll Backer; bro Joshua, sister Sarah Backer, to bro Elisha, to bro Nathaniel. George Partridge guardian to Samll. 11 Jan 1727/8 ord to be rec.
[Lebanon VR: no death record]

[226] [no date] inv of John Lasell [Needham, Mass] decd taken by Nathaniel Reed, Barnard Case. Incl: inkhorn, book. Tot est £53.
[Windham VR: no death recorded]

[227-228] 1 Jan 1727/8 distr of est of Mr Tixwell Ensworth of Canterbury decd done by Samll Butt, ____ Tracy, John Felch. To widow Mrs Sarah Ensworth; to ____ Mr Thomas Ensworth; eld dau Mrs Sarah Cleveland; 2nd dau Mrs Elizabeth White. To widow Great Bible.

[229-230] 2-6 Oct 1727 inv of Deacon Jacob Warren of Plainfield decd taken by John Crery, Ephraim Kingsbury, Daniel Lawrence. Incl Bible and many books. Tot est £750.
[Plainfield VR:1:41 Deacon Jacob Warren d. 3 Sep 1727]

[231-232] 7 Aug 1727 Samuel Adams of Canterbury, yeoman "sick and weak in body." To son Henry Adams; to all grandchildren alive at my death; to four daus; to three sons; to seven children; son Thomas; dau Abigail (if she has children), to dau Margaret (if she has children); son Joseph is sole exec. Wit: Solomon Tracy, Sylvanus "O" Harris, Th____ Fitch. Testator marks: Samuel "X" Adams
[Canterbury VR:1:66 Samuel Adams d. 26 Nov 1727]

Windham (Conn.) Probate Records, Vol 1, Sect.1 (1719-1734)

[233] 18 Sep 1727 inv of est of Samuel Davis decd taken by Henry Green and Benjamin Bixby. 18 Jun 1729 addition made by Sarah Davis, admin.

[234] 30 Oct 1727 inv of Mr Samuel Lee taken by Simon Bryant, Mr Henry Green, Mr James Levens, all of Killingly. Incl: books. Tot est £225.
[Killlingly VR: no death record]

[235] 8 Nov 1727 inv of Mr Samuel Cleveland Jr of Canterbury taken by Benjamin Fasset, Joseph Williams, John Felch. Incl: book, joyner tools, turners tools, gun, dagger, powder horns, bullet pouch, carpenter tools, coopers tools, inkhorn, spectacles. Tot £865.10.10.
[Canterbury VR:1:117 Samuel Cleveland d 1 Oct 1727]

[236-240] Jan 1727/8 inv of Rev. Mr Samll Estabrook of Canterbury, decd taken by Joseph Adams, Deliverance Brown. Incl: two trunks for children, small looking glass, silk blankets for a child and slaves, four golden rings, bond from Joseph Jones and from Thomas Wood. Tot est: £1350. 14 Jul 1729 addition by admin John Fiske, Elea__ Williams.
[Canterbury VR:1:137 Rev Samuel Estabrook d. 26 Jun 1727]

[241-242] [no date] inv of Mr Estabrook's Library

[243-245] blank pages.

[246-247] will of John Sprague [town not given] "lived to see all my children married and settled." To wife Mrs Lois Sprague from before marriage; to grdau Mary Way providing she live with me or my wife until age 18; son Ephraim Sprague; wife sole exec. Wit: Thomas Edgecombe, Elias Frink, Thomas Lothrop. 18 Mar [1727]/1728 Mr Thomas

Windham (Conn.) Probate Records, Vol 1, Sect.1 (1719-1734)

Lothrop and Mr Thomas Edgecombe wit oath in Norwich. 2 May 1728 ord rec.
[Lebanon VR:1:280 Lt John Sprague d. 6 Mar 1727/8]

[247-248] 5 Apr 1728 Lebanon inv of Lt John Sprague of Lebanon decd by Simon Newcomb, Joseph Phelps. Incl one sword, books, two bibles. Tot est £150.

[248-249] 27 Apr 1728 Canterbury inv of Stephen Frost of Canterbury decd. Incl: spectacles, 13 books, carpenters tools, a share in a saw mill. Total est: £462. 15 May 1728 rec. 12 May 1730 addition by Stephen Frost, admin.
[Canterbury VR:1:147 Stephen Frost d. 12 Mar 1728]

[250-251] 15 Mar 1727/8 will of John Stevens of Plainfield "sick and weak in body." To wife Elizabeth; if child she now goes with is a son the two sons split the land; two daus: Mary and Ruth. Son John to pay Mary at 18 or marriage; youngest son to pay Ruth when he is 21. Exec: wife and Ephraim Kingsbury. Wit: Thomas Stevens, Thomas Williams, Ruth "X" Stevens. Testator marks "X" 6 May 1728 wit oath to Ens. John Stevens. 6 May 1728 ord rec.
[Plainfield VR: no death recorded]

[252-253] 19 Mr 1727/8 distr of John Lovejoy of Plainfield decd by Ephraim Kingsbury, John Parkhurst, Samll Sterns. To widow Bathsheba; to eld dau Elizabeth Lovejoy; 2nd dau Ann; 3rd dau Naomi (Bible and books); youngest dau Freelove. To eldest son Benjamin Lovejoy, to youngest son Richard Lovejoy. 6 May 1728 ord rec.
[Plainfield VR: no death recorded]

[254-255] 18 Jun 1728 pursuant to court order of 12 Jun 1728, John Fellows, Ebenezer Harris, Phillip Bump distr, the est of Mr James Welch of Plainfield, decd. To Mrs Marcy

Windham (Conn.) Probate Records, Vol 1, Sect.1 (1719-1734)

Welch, widow; to James Welch, eldest son; to Samuel Welch 2nd son; to Elizabeth Lawrence eldest dau; to Marcy Spaulding 2nd dau; to Martha Welch 3rd dau; to Ebenezer and John Welch, sons.

[256] Samuel Welch of Voluntown; Thomas Welch of Windham, Daniel Lawrence of Killingly and Thomas Spaulding of Plainfield all appeared in court re James Welch's est.

[257] 27 Jun 1728 inv of Robert Badcock of Windham decd taken by Lt Jeremiah Ripley, John Ripley. Tot: 370.11.04.
[Windham VR: no death record]

[258-259] 14 Sep 1724 will of John Rood of Windham "sick and weak in body." Dau Sarah Hall, dau Mary Hebard, dau Constant Fuller, son John Rood, son Thomas Rood; dau Christian Flint decd to her children; Exec: wife Sarah, son John. Mentions wife's children and grandchildren. Wit: Jonathan Crane, Joseph Hebard, Richard Abbe. Testator marks.
[Windham VR: no death recorded]

[259] 27 Jun 1728 wit oath. 27 Jun 1728 will exh and ord rec.

[260] [undated] inv of John Rood Sr who died 4 Mar 1727/8 taken by Jonathan Crane, Joseph Bingham. Incl old Bible and books.

[261-262] 8 May 1725 will of Stephen Tilden of Lebanon "weak of body." wife Mary; son Stephen Tilden, sole exec; dau Hannah Tilden; dau Mary Powell; grandson Joshua Tilden my smith shop tools. Wit: Caleb Pierce, Seth Sutton, Joseph

Windham (Conn.) Probate Records, Vol 1, Sect.1 (1719-1734)

Fowler. Testator signs. 27 Jun 1728 wit oath; 27 Jun 1728 will exh and ord rec.
[Lebanon VR: no death recorded]

[263-264] 19 Oct 1728 inv of Stephen Tilden of Lebanon decd taken by Thomas Hunt, Gershom Clark. Incl: blacksmith tools, hour glass. Total est £950.

[265] 18 Nov 1727 addition to est of Deacon Jacob Warren of Plainfield, decd. taken by John Creery, Ephraim Kingsbury, Daniel Lawrence. Incl 3 books.

[265] 11 Jul 1728 another addition by Ephraim Kingsbury, John Crery, Joseph Warren, admin.

[266-267] 25 Jul 1728 will of Hosea Joyce of Mansfield, yeoman "very sick and weak in body." To brother Thomas Storrs "everything" ... he to pay my two brothers Samuel Joyce and Thomas Joyce; sisters Martha Godfrey, Dorcas House, Mary Parker, Dorothy Oats, Lydia House. Thomas Storrs is sole exec. Wit: Eleazer Williams, Josiah Conant, Jonathan Cross. Testator signs. 5 Aug 1728 with oath. 6 Aug 1728 will exh and ord rec.
[Mansfield VR (Dimmock, 330) Hosea Joyce d. 27 Jul 1728]

[267] 21 Oct 1728 Solomon Hill ack rcpt for his wife Mary from mother Mary Button and brother Peter Button.

[267] 11 Nov 1728 Matthias Button ack rcpt from his mother Mary Button and brother Peter Button. Wit: Samuel Sterns, Sarah Marsh.

[268-269] [undated] inv of James Pinno of Lebanon, decd taken by John "I" Sullard, John Newcomb. Incl: Bible, books, gun, sword. Tot £614.9.2.

Windham (Conn.) Probate Records, Vol 1, Sect.1 (1719-1734)

[Lebanon VR: no death recorded]

[269-270] 11 Nov 1727 Mr Ebenezer Whitney [of Pomfret] decd taken by Benjamin Fassett, Edward Spaulding, Henry Smith. Incl: Bible, books, one quarter of a sawmill. 29 Nov 1728 addition by Anna "O" Whitney, admin. [undated[Henry Smith and Richard Spaulding give to the widow and her children.
[Pomfret VR:1:46 Ebenezer Whitney d. 5 Aug 1727]

[271-272] 20 Aug 1728 inv of Hosea Joyce of Mansfield decd taken by John Arnold, Nathaniel Southworth. Incl a gun. Tot est £820.

[273] [undated] inv of John Brown of Canterbury decd taken by Samuel Coy, John Baldwin. Incl one psalm book. Tot est £145. 13 Jan 1728/9 recorded. 14 Jul 1741 an addition to Mr John Brown's est by Abigail White, adm.
[Canterbury VR: no death recorded]

[274-277] 11 Jan 1728/9 distr of est of Samuel Storrs of Mansfield decd. Widow Martha, eld son Samuel Storrs; Hudgens Storrs; Joseph Storrs; dau Martha Badcock; dau Elizabeth Storrs; dau Mary Jacobs; son John Storrs.

[277] 14 Jan 1728/9 Mr Samuel Storrs to pay Elizabeth Storrs dau of decd.

[278] 14 Jan 1728/9 John Storrs of Mansfield mentioned; Joseph Jacobs Jr and wife mentioned; Mr John Badcock, gdn for his children: Josiah, John, Martha Badcock heirs to Martha his late wife dau of the decd.

Windham (Conn.) Probate Records, Vol 1, Sect.1 (1719-1734)

[279] 18 Sep 1728 inv of Ebenezer Green [of Killingly] taken by Eleazer Bateman, James Levens. Incl: gun, books, one quarter of a sawmill. Tot £184.
[Killingly VR: no death record]

[279] 25 Oct 1727 inv of Jabez Allen [no town given] decd taken by Eleazer Bateman, Benjamin Bixbe. Incl: armor, books, husbandry tools. Tot £650.

[280-282] 27 Dec 1728 will of James Danielson of Killingly, yeoman. Wife Mary; son Samll Danielson; son James Danielson; grandson James Danielson bring him up to college to be prepared by his father and my friend Ebenezer Williams. Exec: son Samuel Danielson. Wit: Ebenezer Williams; Mary Danielson, Frances Caswell.. Testator signs. [undated] witness oath. 11 Feb 1728/9 will exh and ord rec.
[Killingly VR: no death record]

[282] 24-25 Apr 1728 inv of Mr John Stevens of Plainfield decd taken by Samuel Sterns, William Marsh Jr, John Crery. Incl: books, tobacco box, gun, looking glass. Tot est £950.

[283-284] [undated] inv of Mr Samuel Adams of Canterbury decd taken by Solomon Tracy, Nathaniel Robbins, John Felch. Incl: fish spear, money scales, dagger. Est tot £661. 20 Feb 1728/9 recorded.

[285] 22 Jan 1728/9 inv of widow Hannah Rigbe of Plainfield decd taken by Ephraim Kingsbury, Daniel Lawrence, Samll Spaulding. Incl: old Bible, books. Set out for support for "child" and "Indian girll"
[Plainfield VR:1:47 Hannah Wright d.16 Dec 1728]

Windham (Conn.) Probate Records, Vol 1, Sect.1 (1719-1734)

[286] 23 Jan 1728/29 at Pomfret James Danielson ack rcpt from brother Samll Danielson from my father's will. Wit: Ebenezer Williams, Daniel Waters.

[286] 5 Feb 1728/9 at Killingly James Danielson ack rcpt same as above.

[287] 13 Feb 1728/9 inv of Anne Lovejoy of Plainfield, decd taken by Ephraim Kingsbury, John Parkhurst. Incl: gun, land from her father's estate.

[288] 8 Apr 1729 Court appts Mr Henry Smith of Canterbury gdn to Ebenezer Whitney minor son of Ebenezer Whitney of Pomfret, decd.

[288] 8 Apr 1729 Court appts Mr Joseph Adams of Pomfret gdn to Anna Whitney minor dau of Ebenezer Whitney of Pomfret, decd.

[288] 8 Apr 1729 Mr Ezekal eldest son of Mr Ebenezer Whitney of Pomfret decd. Israel Whitney son of Ebenezer Whitney also mentioned.

[289] 8 Apr 1729 Zachariah Whitney is a son of Mr Ebenezer Whitney of Pomfret decd; also Enoch Whitney.

[289-293] 24 Mar 1729 distribution of est of Mr Ebenezer Whitney of Pomfret decd was ordered 27 Nov 1728. Distributors: Benjamin Fassett, Leicester Grosvenor, Deliverance Brown. To Mrs Anna Whitney, relict; eldest son Ezekiel, Zachariah Whitney 2nd son; Ebenezer Whitney youngest son; Enoch 3rd son; Anna Whitney dau gets Bible and books; Israel Whitney 4th son.

Windham (Conn.) Probate Records, Vol 1, Sect.1 (1719-1734)

[294-295] 30 Jul 1728 Josiah Conant, Richard Abbe, Stephen Strong appt 26 Jul 1728 to distribute land in Lebanon to Stephen Tilden; Rowland Powell and Mary his wife; Caleb Pierce and Hannah his wife. Was est of Mr Stephen Tilden decd.

[295] Hudgens Storrs mentioned. Rec 11 Mar 1728/9.

[296-298] Dist. of est of Samuel Storrs of Mansfield by Thomas Storrs, Josiah Conant. Widow Martha Storrs; Samll Storrs eldest son; John Storrs 2nd son; Hudgens Storrs 3rd son; Joseph Storrs 4th son; heirs of Martha Badcock eldest dau; Elizabeth Storrs 2nd dau; Mary Jacobs 3rd dau. Rec 11 Mar 1729.

[299] inv of Gershom Hall of Mansfield decd taken by Thomas Storrs, Josiah Conant. Incl powder horn and powder and shot; frame of a small house; 3000 chestnut shingles. Rec 2 Jul 1729.
[Mansfield VR (Dimmock): no death record.

[300] Tamerson More relict of William More late of Windham decd ack rcpt from exec Joshua More. Wit: John Fitch, Joshua Flint. She marks "O"

[301] 10 Jun 1729 Mr John Dyer of Canterbury is gdn to Jonathan Carver, David Carver, Hannah Carver minor sons and dau of Mr David Carver of Canterbury, decd.

[301] 8 Jul 1729 Mr Samuel Carver eldest son of Mr David Carver of Canterbury decd mentioned.

[301] 9 Jul 1729 Mr Solomon Paine of Canterbury gdn for Benjamin Carver minor son.

Windham (Conn.) Probate Records, Vol 1, Sect.1 (1719-1734)

[301-306] 24 Apr 1728 div of est of Mr David Carver of Canterbury decd by Joseph Adams, John Felch, Solomon Tracy. To widow; to Mrs Sarah Payne, eldest dau; to Hannah Carver youngest dau; to Samuel Carver, eldest son; to Jonathan Carver 2nd son; to David Carver 3rd son; to Benjamin Carver youngest son. 8 Jul 1729 ord rec.

[307] 8 Jul 1729 Court grants Mr Solomon Payne, admin of est of Mr David Carver of Canterbury decd a Quietus est.

[307-308] 14 Jan 1728/9 division of est of Samll Manning Jr decd by Samll Palmer, John Spencer, Eleazer Cary. To Abigail Manning, to Sarah Manning, to Josiah Manning, to Hezekiah Manning, to Samuel Manning, to David Manning. 3 Jul 1729 distr. exh and ord rec. 3 Jul 1729 Samll Manning is gdn of Josiah Manning minor son of Samuel Manning decd.

[310-312] 22 Jun 1727 will of Samuel Estabrook, clerk. To wife Rebecca Estabrook, sole exec receives all until children come of age; she to ask advice of my friends Mr Fiske of Killingly, Mr Williams of Pomfret; and Justice Adams of this place in the selling of any real estate. To son Nehemiah Estabrook; son Hobart Estabrook to be brought up to college; dau Mary Estabrook. Test. signs. Wit: Ebenezer Williams, Daniel Kirtland, Richard Pollet. Rev. Mr Daniel Kirtland and Richard Pollet wit oath. 30 Nov 1727 Rev. Mr Ebenezer Williams wit oath. 15 Jul 1729 will exh and ord rec.

[312-313] 25 Dec 1727 will of William Rogers of Voluntown "weak in body." To eldest son John; 2nd son William; son Matthew Patrick and my dau Elizabeth his wife; dau Anna; dau Janet. Wife Janet sole exec to be advised by Mr John Dixon and Mr Robert Park. Wit: Joseph Gallup, Benjamin Gallup, Samuel Dorrance. Testator signs. 8 Jul 1729 John

Windham (Conn.) Probate Records, Vol 1, Sect.1 (1719-1734)

Gallup and Benjamin Gallup wit oath. 28 Jul 1729 will exh and ord rec.
[Voluntown VR: no death record]

[314-315] 3 Sep 1728 inv of William Brewster of Lebanon decd by Ebenezer West, Benjamin Brewster. Incl seven books and a gun. Tot est £180 no land. [undated] Ebenezer West and Benjamin Brewster state there is nothing left in inv for support of widow, recommend £10 money.
[Lebanon VR:1:22 William Brewster d. 11 Aug 1728]

[316-319] 25 Apr 1729 agreement to distr est of William Brewster of Lebanon decd. Patience Brewster widow; William Brewster of Mansfield; Samuel Brewster; Joseph Trumbull Jr atty for Ebenezer Brewster; Peter Brewster of Lebanon; Matthew Dwolfe of Bolton in behalf of his wife Patience. Wit: John Woodward, Sarah Woodward, Stephen Powell, Ebenezer Gray, Israel Woodward, John Crery, Gershom Clark.

[319-322] 22 Mar 1728/9 will of James Kidder of Mansfield "being sick and weak in body." Wife Mary; son James sole exec; son John; son Nathaniel; son Ephraim; son Joseph; eldest dau Elizabeth; dau Hannah under 18; dau Sarah under 18. If James refused exec then son John. Wit: Thomas Storrs, Elisha Dunham, Ebenezer "his mark" Fenton. Testator signs. 2 Jul 1729 Capt Thomas Storrs and Elisha Dunham wit oath. 2 Jul 1729 Mr James Kidder refuses exec and John Kidder accepted.
[Mansfield VR (Dimmock, 331) James Kidder Sr d. 18 May 1729]

[322] 7 Jun 1729 at Mansfield inv of James Kidder, decd taken by Thomas Storrs, Josiah Conant, Sheber Hall. Incl: horn, powder, Bible, book. Total est £216.

Windham (Conn.) Probate Records, Vol 1, Sect.1 (1719-1734)

[323-326] 21 Jan 1726/7 will of Benjamin Woodworth of Lebanon "being very sick and weak in body." To eldest son Benjamin Woodworth; sons Benjamin, Ichabod, Ebenezer, Amos, Ezekiel, and Caleb. Daus: Deborah Sprague, Hannah Walar, Ruth Owen, Judith Newcombe, Margaret Owen, Priscilla Fuller; children of Elizabeth Southard decd; children of Mary Sprague decd. Mentions land in Seconet, Bristol Co MA. Benjamin is sole exec. Wit: Thomas Root, Nathaniel Dewey, John Woodward. 20 Jun 1728 Thomas Root wit oath; 27 Jun 1729 John Woodward Esq with oath; 3 Jul 1729 will exh and ord rec.
[Lebanon VR:1:340 Benjamin Woodworth father of Ichabod d. 22 Apr 1729]

[327-329] Lebanon inv of Benjamin Woodworth of Lebanon decd taken by Joseph Marton, Samll Wright. Incl: sermon book, old Bible, books. Tot est: £120. 3 Sep 1729 addition of £27.

[329-330] 29 Mar 1729 will of William Moore of Windham "very sick and weak in body." Wife: Tamerson; dau Elizabeth; dau Experience; dau Martha; two grandchildren: Mary Badcock and Jonathan Badcock when they come of age or marry; son Joshua is sole exec. Wit: John Fitch, Joshua Flint, Abraham Mitchell. Testator marks "X" 2 Jul 1729 wit oath. 2 Jul 1729 will exh and ord rec.
[Windham VR no death record]

[331-332] 3 May 1729 inv of William Moore of Windham decd taken by John Fitch, Joshua Flint. Incl powder box, old Bible, books, a Great Bible, a looking glass. Tot est £810.

[[333-338] 12 Feb 1721/2 will of Peter Thatcher of Milton, Suffolk Co, Mass, clerk, "being in a compitent mesure of

Windham (Conn.) Probate Records, Vol 1, Sect.1 (1719-1734)

Bodily health." Wife Susannah property she owned before we were married; ratify marriage contract; land she purchased in Dorchester and in Milton and in Conn; also "ston" ring which my former wife gave me "ye pose of wch ring In her posesion Is all love ever Fresh and sparkling." Eldest son Oxenbridge Thatcher land in White & Alley in Coleman St, St Stephan Parish, London, England. Children: Peter Thatcher, clerk, and Theodea Gulliver and my grandchildren of my dau Niles, decd—Elizabeth, Sarah, Samuel, Mary, Nathaniel. Son: Thomas Thatcher; eldest son Peter Thatcher. Library to sons Oxenbridg and Peter equally. To wife: "my Negro Woman Hagar sent me by sister Scot from Jameco and at my Wife's Deth I give her time if she Desires to be free." "Item I give and bequeath little Samboo my Negro servant born in my house" to son Peter "(beleving he Will be kind to him)" Brother Ralph Thatcher. To Capt Gulliver. Martha Oxenbridge's estate in Barbados. Exec: son Oxenbridge and son Peter. Wit: Samuel Hascall, Ephraim Tucker, Neh. Clap. Testator signs. 8 Jan 1727/8 will exh and ord rec.

[339-340] 8 Aug 1724 will of Susannah Thatcher of Milton [Mass] wife of Peter Thatcher of Milton "Bodyly Weakness." Will made with approbation of my husband Mr Peter Thatcher, clerk. Kinsman: Mr John Bailey in Boston my silver tankard wthat has his arms on it. Sister: Madam Rebecca Brown. Kinswoman: Mrs Margaret Pain. Son Oxenbridge; dau Gulliver and her ch. Jonathan and Jerusha Gulliver; granddau Elizabeth Hayward; ch of dau Niles: Samuel, Sarah, Mary, and Nathaniel Niles. Niece: Elizabeth Ellison; nieces Anna and Comfort Ellison; kinswoman Susannah Glover... her ch before her decease. To Hagar my Negro Woman 40sh; to Margaret Natahank 40sh; to Jonathan Thomas 20sh; to Sambo, Jenny, and Hagar 10 sh each. Exec: husband and sons Peter and Oxenbridge. Wit: Ephraim Tucker, Nathaniel Clapp, Lydey Clapp. Testator signs.

Windham (Conn.) Probate Records, Vol 1, Sect.1 (1719-1734)

[341-343] 25 Jul 1728 will of Richard Dresser of Killingly. Wife Mary; son Jacob under 21; dau Mary Hallwell; children: Martha Dresser; Richard Dresser, John Dresser, Joseph Dresser, Asa Dresser, Abigail Dresser, Benjamin Dresser, Keziah Dresser. Exec: wife and sons Jacob, Richard and Joseph. Wit: Jonathan Eaton, John Dwight, Samson Howe. 8 Jul 1729 wit oath. 8 Jul 1729 will exh and ord rec.
[Killingly VR: no death record]

[344] 27 Jan 1728/9 inv of Richard Dresser [res] adjacent to Killingly decd by Benjamin Bixby, Samson Howe. Incl: armor, no land. Tot est £243.

[345] 9 Aug 1728 inv of Bartholomew Williams of Plainfield decd taken by Samuel Sterns, James Marsh. Incl a pocket book. Tot est £16.
[Plainfield VR:1:44 Bartholome[w] Williams d. 24 Apr 1728]

[345-347] 16 Oct 1727 inv of Josiah Spaulding of Plainfield decd taken by Ephraim Kingsbury, Thomas Stevens Jr, Samll Sterns. Set aside for family's use: £35.18.0. Incl books, best gun and ammunition, old gun, homestead of his father, tanning supplies, "one half of a Dear skin sent to newtown to sell." Tot est L1546
[Plainfield VR:1:41 Josiah Spaulding d. 21 Sep 1727]

[348] 5 Dec 1728 Killingly inv of Jacob Spaulding decd taken by Ebenezer Brooks, Thomas Gould, Josiah Procter. Tot est £656. One year provisions set aside for family.
[Killingly VR:1:5 Jacob Spaulding d. 24 Sep 1728]

[349] 9 Jul 1729 inv of William Rogers of Voluntown decd by Ephraim Kingsbury, Robert "X" Williams. Two Bibles and a psalter. Tot est £55.

Windham (Conn.) Probate Records, Vol 1, Sect.1 (1719-1734)

[Voluntown: no death record]

[350] 5 Dec 1729 Daniel Lamb and Zerviah Lamb ack rcpt of £30 from our Brother Peter Button of Plainfield from the est of our father Matthias Button of Plainfield decd. Wit: Jacob Lamb, Jerusha "X" Lamb.

[351-352] 22 Jan 1729 will of Benjamin Daffty [i.e. Daughty or Duffy] of Windham "weak low condition of body in frailty and that I must By this sickness be brought to my grave." Wife Elizabeth; four daus Desire, Elizabeth, Margaret, and Martha. exec: wife and brother Bernard Case and Jacob Lilly. Wit: Jonah Palmer, Benjamin Case, Ebenezer Hebard. Testator marks. 3 Feb 1729/30 wit oath. 3 Feb 1729/30 will exh and ord rec.
[Windham VR: no death record]

[353-354] 11 Aug 1728 will of Joseph Eaton of Killingworth "very sick and weak in body." Wife Hannah sole exec. Seven children: Sarah, Catherine, Hanna, Mary, Desire, Joseph and Marchont. Wit: Josiah Stevens, Nathaniel Nott, Samll Wilcox Jr. Testator marks. 13 Feb 1729/30 wit oath. 3 Mar 1730 will exh/ord rec.

[354-355] 12 Feb 1729/30 inv of Joseph Eaton of Killingworth decd taken by Josiah Stevens, Samll Wilcox Jr. Incl: one large gun, seven old books, looking glass, a bag of feathers. Total est £11. 2 Mar 1729/30 add to inv by Isaac Crane, Jonathan Read. 26 Jan 1741 add to inv by Hannah Eaton exec (she signs)

[356] 19 Feb 1729/30 inv of Deacon Thomas Bingham of Windham decd taken by Richard Abbe and Jonathan Huntington of sd Windham. Tot est £100.

Windham (Conn.) Probate Records, Vol 1, Sect.1 (1719-1734)

[Windham VR:1:37 Deacon Thomas Bingham d. 16 Jan 1729/30 aet. about 88 years.

[357-8] 29 Jan 1729/30 will of Thomas Grosvenor of Pomfret, yeoman. Wife Elizabeth. Eldest son is under 21. Brethren: Leicester Grosvenor and Ebenezer Grosvenor. Children (all Grosvenor): William, Amos, Joshua, Elizabeth. Exec: wife and two brothers. Testator signs. Wit: Ebenezer Williams, Jehosophat Holmes, Joseph Tucker. 3 Mar 1729/30 Pomfret Mr Ebenezer Williams, clerk and Joseph Tucker, yeoman wit oath. 7 Mar 1729/30 will exhibited and ordered recorded.
[Pomfret VR:1:21 Thomas Grosvenor d. 6 Feb 1729]

[359] 5-6 Mar 1729/30 inv of Thomas Grosvenor of Pomfret decd by Jacob Wilson, Jonathan Dresser, Nehemiah Sabin. Incl land in Killingly. Tot est: £2500. Provisions made for children.

[360-361] [undated] Inv of Benjamin Daffty [Daughty Doughty Duffy] of Windham decd by Jonah Palmer, Joshua Lasell, Ebenezer Hebard. Incl: gun, sword and belt, ammunition, silver buttons, 20 pounds of tobacco. Tot est £315. Rec 17 Jun 1730.

[362-363] 10 Feb 1729/30 inv of Elisha Dunham of Mansfield decd taken by Thomas Storrs, Ebenezer Dunham. Incl: 3 wigs, gun and 2 powder horns, bullets, a Bible, books. Total est £610.
[Mansfield VR (Dimmock) no death record]

[364] 16 Jun 1730 inv of David Dill [of Voluntown] decd taken by Nathaniel Juel and Thomas Stevens Jr Tot est £240. 8 Aug 1738 add by Mary "X" Dill, admin.
[Voluntown VR: no death record]

Windham (Conn.) Probate Records, Vol 1, Sect.1 (1719-1734)

[365] 28 Apr 1730 add to est of Gershom Hall of Mansfield decd by Thomas Storrs, Josiah Conant.

[365] 1 Jun 1727 Lydia "L" Lillie ack rcpt of her share of her father George Lillie decd est from her gdn and uncle Jonathan Silsby.

[366] 23 Mar 1721 Windham Elizabeth "E" Lillie ack rcp from her bro Jacob Lillie her part of her father's est.

[366] 23 Mar 1721 Windham Jonathan Silsby ack rcpt from Jacob Lillie admin of George Lille of Windham decd of Bethiah Lillie's portion of her father's estate.

[367] 23 Mar 1721 Elisha Little ack rcpt from Jacob Lillie admin of my father George Lillie est.

[367] 23 Mar 1721 Mary Lillie ack rcpt from bro Jacob Lillie admin of my father George Lillie est.

[367] 14 Jul 1730 Reuben Lillie ack rcpt from bro Jacob Lillie admin of my father George Lillie est.

[368-369] Canterbury inv of John Pike of Canterbury decd taken by Benjamin Fasset, Thoms Brown, Joseph Adams. Incl: "Jury handled knife and fork," tobacco, fowling piece, musket, carbine, small gun, Bible, books. Tot est £163.
[Canterbury VR: no death record]

[370-371] 18 Apr 1729 will of Robert Mason of Ashford, taylor "having a very bad cancer in my face and knowing not how it may prove." Wife Hannah sole exec all for 13 years. The eldest son Robert Mason gets double share and other ch get single share. Wit: Isaac Kendall, Josiah Bugbee, Samuel

Snow Jr. Testator signs. 23 Sep 1730 wit oath. 23 Sep 1730 will exh and ord recorded.
[Ashford VR: no death record]

[372-376] 24 Mar 1728 will of Mary Saltonstall of Boston "in good health." To eld son of my late husband Gurdon Saltonstall Esq—Mr Roswell Saltonstall a silver bowl; to son Nathaniel Saltonstall large silver porringer; to Gurdon Saltonstall 2 small silver salvers; to Elizabeth Christophers and Sarah Davis; to Mary Miller; To Katherine Battle [dau of Gurdon Saltonstall Esq?]; to the four daus of my decd husband; to children of my late brother Richard Whittingham Esq my est in Great Britain; to my sister Mrs Elizabeth Payson and her son Samll Appleton and her dau Elizabeth Payson; my sister Mrs Martha Rogers and to her sons viz John, Nathaniel, Richard, Daniel, and Samll; to my b-i-l Rev Mr Payson and Rev Mr Rogers; to Mr Joseph Brandon and his wife Mrs Martha Brandon; to my niece Mrs Hannah Willard [items] left to me by my husband William Clark Esq... also my negroes; to Josiah Willard Esq; to Capt Jonathan Clark; to Mr William Ho[lb]arton; to Mrs Sarah Brandon; to poor of the town of Boston also to poor of "new old south church;" to ministers of sd church viz Rev Mr Joseph Sewall and Rev Mr Thomas Prince; to Harvard College in Cambridge; £500 for burial "without any pomp" and rings and gloves to all ministers in town; to Richard, Thomas, Mary, Elizabeth Clark the four younger ch of my nephew William Clark; to Josiah and Hannah Willard my nieces ch by Josiah Willard Esq; to William Clark eld son to above William Clark and Hannah his wife a farm in Pomfret and a large silver bown with a cover I had from the estate of my grandfather John Lawrence Esq; two sister and niece Hannah Willard and their children receive remainer (5-7000 acres); nephew Mr Samuel Appleton; Rev Mr Coleman and brick south church; seven ch of my late husb to receive all estate left to me by my late husband; Rev Mr

Windham (Conn.) Probate Records, Vol 1, Sect.1 (1719-1734)

John Rogers of Ipswich, my b-i-l Mr Joseph Brandon, Mrs Hannah Willard and Mr William Clark (Mrs Willards eld son) appt execs. Wit: Nathll Goodwin, Benja Babbidge, John Roydell at Concord. Testator signs. Probated Boston 16 Jan 1729. 11 Jan 1730/1 1100 acres of Madam Mary Saltonshall appraised at £800 by Henry Cobb, Richard Adams.

[377-380] 28 Feb 1728/9 will of Nathaniel Jewel of Plainfield, yeoman. To wife Sarah 1/3 of all except husbandry, tacking, and smithing tools; to two sons Joshua and David (who is under 21) smith shop; to son Nathaniel ½ smith tools; to dau Mary Juell at 21 or marriage; to dau Sarah Juell at 21 or marriage; to dau Abigail under 21 or marriage; to dau Hannah at 21 or marriage. Selects Mr Joseph Lawrence, Mr David Whitney, and Mr Ebenezer Williams (or any two of them) to distr est; appts wife and brother-in-law David Whitney execs. Testator signs. Wit: Ephraim Fellows, Isaac Fellows, John Crery. 29 Sep 1730 wit oath; 29 Sep 1730 will exh and ord recorded.
[Plainfield VR: no death recorded]

[381-383] 15,16,22 Sep 1730 inv of Mr Nathaniel Jewel of Plainfield decd by David Lawrence, Joseph Lawrence, and Thomas Stevens Jr. Incl; one gun, 2 looms, two Bibles, 11 books, smith tools.

[384-386] 10 Sep 1730 will of Jonah Palmer of Windham "weak in boddy." To son Jonathan Palmer; son Gershom Palmer; son Elihu Palmer; grandchildren Ruth Read, Mehetabel Read, Jonathan Read, Solomon Read and David Read (not of age); dau Elizabeth Spencer wife of John Spencer gristmill; dau Hannah Read wife of John Read; dau Deborah Palmer; Exec: son-in-law John Spencer. Testator signs. Wit: John Fitch, Jeremiah Ripley, Richard Abbe. 28 Sep 1730 Mr John Fitch Esq, Lt Jeremiah Ripley, and Richard Abbe wit

oath. 30 Oct 1730 will exh and ord rec. 22 Dec 1730 recorded.
[Windham VR:A:30 Jonah Palmer d. 19 Sep 1730 ae 68]

[387] 16 Oct 1730 inv of Jonah Palmer of Windham decd taken by Richard Abbe, Jonathan Huntington. Tot est £85. 23 Feb 1731/2 add to above by exec John Spencer.

[388] 5 Oct 1730 inv of movable est of Robert Mason of Ashford decd by Isaac Kendall, Josiah Bugbee, Samll Snow Jr. 5 Jan 1730/1 recorded.

[389-390] 3 Dec 1730 inv of Benjamin Scott of Windham decd. Incld: sawmill. Tot est £525. 12 Jan 1730/1 rec.
[Windham VR: no death recorded]

[391-393] 17 Sep 1730 will of Ebenezer Grosvenor of Pomfret, yeoman. Wife Ann; dau Susannah under 21 and unmarried; son John; sons Ebenezer and Caleb; mother [no name given]; brother Leicester Grosvenor and wife execs. Wit: Nehemiah Sabin; John Williams; Ebenezer Holbrook. Testator signs. Woodstock 27 Oct 1730 wit oath before John Chandler JP. 10 Nov 1730 ord rec. 8 Feb 1730/1 recorded.
[Pomfret VR:1:7 Ebenezer Grosvenor d. 20 Sep 1730]

[393-395] [undated] inv of Ebenezer Grosvenor of Pomfret decd taken by Nehemiah Sabin, Samll Holdridge, Seth Pain. Tot est £4950. 8 Feb 1730/1 rec. 12 Jan 1730/1 addition by Ann Grosvenor exec.

[396-398] 2 Aug 1728 John Broughton of Windham "weak in body." Son John Broughton; son Samuel; dau Elizabeth Fuller; dau Hannah Ballard; dau Chester [sic] Brown; dau Mehitabel Fuller; dau Abigail Broughton; son Thomas; wife Hannah. Hannah and Thomas execs. Wit: Elizabeth "E"

Windham (Conn.) Probate Records, Vol 1, Sect.1 (1719-1734)

Huntington, Ruth "X" Read, Richard Abbe. Testator signs. 11 Jan 1730/1 wit oath. 20 Jan 1730/1 will exh and ord rec. 9 Feb 1730/1 recorded.
[Windham VR:A:13 John Broughton d. 1 Jan 1730/1 ae 77]

[398-399] 13 Jan 11730/1 inv of John Broughton taken by Richard Abbe, Joseph Huntington Jr, Jonathan Huntington. Tot est £450. 22 Feb 1730/1 rec. 14 Jan 1734/5 addition.

[400] [undated] addition to inv of Mrs Luce of Windham decd by John Spencer, Elihu Parkman. Rec 11 Jan 1731/2.

[401] [undate] inv of John Haskall est [town not given] by Henry Green, John Wiley. Tot est £5. 9 Mar 1731/2 rec.

[401-403] 22 Feb 1730/1 inv of est of Mrs Grace Luce of Windham decd taken by John Spencar, Elihu Parkman. Incl: powder horn, looking glass, old Bible and books. Tot est £25. 22 Jan 1731 [sic] rec.
[Windham VR:1:128 Grace Luce d. 18 May 1730]

[403-404] 22 Jan 1730/1 dist of est of Mr Nathaniel Jewel of Plainfield decd by David Whitney, Joseph Lawrence, Ebenezer Williams. Mrs Sarah Jewel widow; eldest son Nathaniel smith shop. 6 Apr 1731 rec.

[405-406] Windham 10 Sep 1730 inv of est of Ebenezer Hibbard decd taken by Samll Bingham, John Abbe, John Manning who were sworn before Richard Abbe JP. Incl books and Bible. Tot est £600. 6 Apr 1731 rec. 9 Jan 1732/3 addition by Robert Hibbard, Joseph Hibard.
[Windham VR: no death record]

[407-409] 21 Dec 1730 court ordered distribution by Jacob Warren, Ephraim Kingsbury, Daniel Lawrence. Est of

Windham (Conn.) Probate Records, Vol 1, Sect.1 (1719-1734)

Eleanor Shephard relict of Samll Shephard of Plainfield decd. To Jonathan Shephard eld son; David Shephard 2nd son; Nathan Shephard 3rd son; Benjamin Shephard 4th son; Eleanor Darby eld dau; Luce Shephard 3rd dau. Wit: Thomas Gallup, Joseph Lawrence, John Crery.
[Plainfield VR: no death record for Eleanor or Samuel]

[410-417] 4 Feb 1729 William McDowell admin of est of Archibald McDowell requests appraisal. Done by Nathaniel Dean, John "T" Dixson, Daniel Hyde. Incl: one old Bible many books, pages of items suggesting that McDowell was a milliner. Tot est £50 plus £225 debts due. 20 Jul 1731 rec.

[418] 3 Dec 1730 Hepsebah "X" Ballard ack rcpt of her portion of her father Mr William Ballard whose will was dated 21 Jul 1721. Rcvd from brothers Enoch, Peleg, and Thomas Ballard. Wit: Ephraim Kingsbury, John Crery. 13 Aug 1731 rec.

[419-420] 11 May 1731 will of Robert Boswell of Canterbury, yeoman "very sick and weak in body." Land already given to sons Thomas and Moses; wife Mary a good Bible and what she brought to her marriage with me; dau Sarah Cleveland; dau Hannah Cady; dau Mehitabel Boswell. Trusty friend John Felch my sole exec. Testator marks "B" Wit: Joseph Williams, John Bacon, Hezekiah Pollot. 8 Jun 1731 wit oath. 8 Jun 1731 will exh and ord rec. 14 Feb 1731/2 rec.
[Canterbury VR: no death record]

[421-422] 11 Jan 1732/2 will of Edward Walker of Ashford, husbandman "very sick and weak in body." Wife Mary; dau Mary under 18 and unm; exec: wife Mary, Deacon Kendall, Phillip Eastman. Testator signs. Wit: John Perry, Samuel

Windham (Conn.) Probate Records, Vol 1, Sect.1 (1719-1734)

Rice, Francis Pierce. 4 Feb 1731/2 wit oath. 8 Feb 1731/2 will exh and ord rec. 14 Feb 1731/2 rec.
[Ashford VR:1:3 Edward Walker d 13 Jan 1731/2 ae 41 years and about six weeks]

[423] 4 Feb 1731/2 inv of Mr David Walker of Ashford decd taken by John Berry, Samll Rice, Moses Smith. Incl: husbandry tools, carpenters tools. Tot est £550. 14 Feb 1731/2 rec.

[424] 6 Jan 1731/2 inv of Joseph Griffin of Pomfret, husbandman decd by Eleazer Sabin, Jehosophat Holmes, Eleazer Holbrook. Incl: "his negro man servant £80," looking glass. Total £2365.11.10. 14 Feb 1731/2 rec.
[Pomfret VR:1:36 Joseph Griffin d. 3 Dec 1731]

[425] 28 May 1731 inv of Nathan Wright of Ashford who died 20 Nov 1730 taken by John Pitts and Nathaniel "X" Abbott. Incl gun. Tot est £250. 17 Feb 1731/2 rec.
[Ashford VR: no death record]

[426] 9 Nov 1731 Pomfret. William Sharp and John Brooks estimate value of improvements made to farm by Mr Joseph Dene, Mr Ebenezer Holbrook, and Mr Joseph Hamlett, gdns to heirs of Mr William Hamlett decd. Improvements are £70. 9 Nov 1731 oath by William Sharp and John Brooks. 4 Apr 1732 recorded.

[427-428] 16 Sep 1731 Windham. inv of Jonathan Palmer of Windham, decd taken by Richard Abbe, Benjamin Follitt. Incl: books. Tot est £60.

[428] 16 Apr 1731 Windham. Mr Benjamin "X" Luce ack rcpt of £40 from est of Israel Luce of Windham, decd. Wit; John Spencer, Ebenezer Spencer. 9 May 1732 rec.

Windham (Conn.) Probate Records, Vol 1, Sect.1 (1719-1734)

[429-431] 11 Sep 1731 will of William Durk [i.e. Durkee] of Windham. Son William; son Henry; dau Martha Hibbard wife of John Hibbard; dau Jerusha Martin wife of Ebenezer Martin; daus Huldah, Sarah, Hannah, Rebeckah and Lucy Durkee; wife Rebeckah; exec son William and wife. Testator signs. Wit: John Woodward, Richard Abbe, Mary "O" Abbe. 8 Mar 1731/2 wit oath. 13 Mar 1732 will exh and ord rec. 13 May 1732 rec.
[Windham VR:1:25   William Durkee d. 2 Mar 1731/2 ae about 60 years]

[431-432] 8 Mar 1731/2 inv of William Durkee of Windham decd by George Martin, William Durkee, Gideon Cobb. Incl: books. Tot est £175. 22 May 1732 rec.

[433-435] 31 May 1725 will of Thomas Rugg of Lexington, Mass. Wife Elizabeth Rugg; all my children and grch Jacob Waters; dau Sarah Parker; daus Hannah, Abigail and Martha Rugg, and Jacob Waters aforesaid. Sole exec: wife. Appt friends William Monroe, Joseph Wasset and John Laughton overseers. Testator marks "O" Wit: Nathaniel Dunklee, Ebenzer "his mark" Fisk, John Hancock. 31 Dec 1731 wit oath before Francis Bowman JP. 23 Feb 1731/2 Thomas Rugg of Mansfield decd. 23 May 1732 rec.
[Mansfield VR (Dimmock) no death record]

[435-436] 17 Nov 1731 inv of Thomas Rugg of Mansfield decd taken by Joseph Jacobs, Thomas Storrs. Incl: Bible and two books. Tot est £30. 23 May 1732 rec. 23 Jun 1736 Windham addition. 23 Jun 1736 rec.

[437] 11 Mar 1732 inv of Zebulon Abbott of Windham[?] decd taken by Thomas Marsh and Thomas Teasdale [Tisdale] Incl: two Bibles, books. Tot est £400. 20 Jun 1732 rec.

Windham (Conn.) Probate Records, Vol 1, Sect.1 (1719-1734)

[Windham VR:1:62 a Zebediah d. 2 Dec 1731 same?]

[438] 19 Mar 1731 inv of John Chapman of Ashford decd taken by Edward Walker, Benjamin Royse minor. Tot: £142.09.6. 28 May 1731 Benjamin Russell [sic] Jr and Edward Walker make oath before Joseph Levens JP. 19 Jun 1732 rec.
[Ashford VR:1:9 John Chapman d. 23 Jan 1731/2]

[439-440] 4 May 1730 inv of widow Hannah Woodward decd widow and relict of Joseph Woodward of Canterbury decd taken by Jabez Fitch, Peletiah Fitch. Incl Bible and books. 20 Jun 1732 rec.
[Canterbury VR:1:246 Joseph Woodward d. 14 May 1726; no death record for widow]

[440-441#2] 16 Mar 1732 inv of John Stedman of Lebanon decd [died 24 Feb 1731/2] by Zachariah Lumis [i.e. Loomis], Nathll Porter. Incl: an old gun, two Bibles and books, compass, looking glass. Tot est £300. 20 Jun 1732 rec. addition £17.18.9 by Joseph Dewey admin.
[Lebanon VR:1:279 John Stedman d. 23 Feb 1731/2]

[442] 8 May 1728 Ephraim Sprague ack recpt from his mother Lois Sprague. 20 Jun 1732 rec.

[442] 24 Nov 1731 Thomas Bingham and Jabez Bingham of Norwich ch of Thomas Bingham of Norwich decd ack rcpt of grandfather Thomas Bingham of Windham decd. Uncle Jonathan Bingham is admin. Wit: Jonathan Huntington, John D_____.

[443] 24 Nov 1731 Bond of Jonathan Bingham as adm of est of our father Thomas Bingham of Windham decd: Abel Bingham, John Backus, Stephen Tracy, Nathaniel Bingham,

Windham (Conn.) Probate Records, Vol 1, Sect.1 (1719-1734)

Samll Bingham, Stephen Bingham, Joseph Bingham. Wit by Richard Abbe, Jonathan Bingham Jr. Also David Huntington wit by Mary Messenger, Jonathan Bingham Jr; Daniel Mason wit by Thomas Huntington, Ebenezer Lyman; Charles "X" Mudg [i.e. Mudge] wit by Jonathan Bingham Jr, Mary "X" Messenger; Daniel Huntingon wit by Peter "M" Morehouse, Gideon Bingham; Abigail "X" Mason wit by Simon Lathrop, Jonathan Bingham Jr; Thomas Dimmock, no wit. 4 Jul 1732 rec.

[444] Heirs of Robert Badcock. Joseph Swetland and Marcy "M" his wife sign 22 Apr 1730 wit William Swetland and Temperance Swetland; Ebenezer Badcock 6 Mar 1731 wit Samuel Allen, Mary Wood; Daniel Badcock 6 Mar 1731 wit Samuel Allen, Mary Wood; Thankful "+" Porter, Thomas Porter, Joshua More, Dorothy "X" Moore sign 14 Apr 1731 wit Joseph Strong, Benjamin "X" Badcock, Martha "C" Dawson signs 15 Oct 1731 wit John Porter, Joseph Hovey, Daniel Davison. 17 Oct 1731 wit Wade Cross, Joseph Hovey. 4 Jul 1732 rec.

[445] 1 Apr 1732 inv of William Ticknor of Lebanon decd taken by Nathll Gove, Ezekiel Loomis. 12 Jul 1732 rec. [Lebanon VR:1:309 William Tickner d. 2 Mar 1731/2]

[446] 24 Jul 1732 inv of Nathaniel Ayrs [i.e. Ayers] of Voluntown decd taken by Ebenezer Pierce and Manassah Minor. Incl looking glass. Tot est L350. 29 Jul 1732 rec. [Voluntown VR: no death record]

[447] 10 Apr 1732 Ebenezer Holbrook gdn ack rcpt from Mr Joseph Done of Pomfret of est of Mr William Hamlit of Pormfret decd. Wit: John Crery, Elexand Stewart. 14 Nov 1732 rec.

Windham (Conn.) Probate Records, Vol 1, Sect.1 (1719-1734)

[447]   5 Dec 1732   Abigail Cary of Plainfield ack rcpt from Jacob Warren and Abigail Warren admins of est of Joseph Cary Jr of Windham, decd. They being my gdns. Wit: Daniel Lawrence, Daniel Hulit. 9 Apr 1733 rec.
[Windham VR: no death record]

[448-449]   9 Oct 1732   Archibald McDowell of Norwich decd insolvent. Mentions William and Angus McDowell.

[450-453]   31 Jan 1731/2   will of Andrew Warner of Mansfield, yeoman "weak and sick in body." Wife Deborah, son Joseph Warner land in Windham; son Elisha; son Thomas land in Windham. Elisha Warner sole exec and to care for his mother; dau Thankful Huntington; dau Mary Storrs. Wit: Eleazer Williams, Ebenezer Abbe, Joshua Abbe. Testator signs. 9 Jun 1732 wit oath before Thomas Huntington JP. 30 Jun 1732 will exh and ord rec. 10 Jan 1732/3 rec.
[Mansfield (Dimmock) no death record]

[453-454]   30 Oct 1732 inv of Mr Andrew Warner decd taken at Mansfield by Thomas Storrs and John Slapp. Incl: due from Thomas Corbin of Ashford; Great bible, books, guns. Tot est: £430.

[455-456]   9 Aug 1731   will of John Badcock of Windham. Wife Elizabeth all until eld son is 21; son Josiah Badcock, son John Badcock; dau Martha Badcock under 18; son Nathaniel Badcock; child "my wife is bigg with" Wife Elizabeth and brother Thomas Porter execs. Wit: Thomas Porter, Mary "O" Leach, Elizabeth "E" Sessions. 31 Aug 1731 wit oath. 12 Sep 1732 will exh and ord rec. 12 Sep 1732 rec.
[Windham VR:1:114 John Babcock d. 15 Aug 1731]

[457-458]   30 Aug 1731   inv of John Badcock husbandman taken at Windham by Thomas Durkee, Thomas Marsh,

Windham (Conn.) Probate Records, Vol 1, Sect.1 (1719-1734)

Gideon Cobb. Incl: first wife's goods and second wife's goods; guns. Tot est: £520. 12 Sep 1732 rec. 29 Jun 1733 addition by Elizabeth Badcock exec.

[458] 12 Mar 1732/3 inv of Mr Joseph Bugbee of Ashford decd taken by Nathaniel Abbott, Edward Lewis. Tot est: £300. 23 Apr 1733 rec.
[Ashford VR: no death record]

[459] ___ Sept 1727 inv of Nathaniel Barker of Windham decd taken by Thomas Marsh, Paul Holt. Incl a gun.
[Windham VR:1:80 Nathaniel Barker d. 27 Aug 1727 ae about 34 years]

[460] 31 Aug 1732 inv of Henry Farnum decd at Windham by Thomas Marsh, Gideon Cobb. Incl books. Tot est £355. 23 Apr 1733 rec.
[Windham VR:1:131 Henry Farnum d. 25 Jul 1732 ae about 45 years]

[461-463] 6 Mar 1731 will of Jacob Parker of Ashford, cordwainter. Son Jacob Parker sole exec; three ch of dau Eastman; dau Mary Rood; dau Elizabeth Eaton; dau Experience Johnson; dau Patience Greegs [?]; wife Thankful Parker; £10 to Church of God in Ashford. Wit Thomas Corbin, George Chedol, Thomas Tiffany Jr. Testator signs. 14 Mar 1731/2 Mansfield wit oath before Thomas Huntington JP. 13 May 1733 will exh and ord rec. 2 May 1733 [sic] rec.
[Ashford VR: no death record]

[463] 10 Mar 1732/3 Ashford inv of Jacob Parker of Ashford decd taken by John Perry, Phillip Eastman. Tot est: £1100. 2 May 1733 rec.

Windham (Conn.) Probate Records, Vol 1, Sect.1 (1719-1734)

[464] 20 Apr 1733 Killingly inv of Joseph Covell by Henry Green, Isaac Cutler, Ebenezer Bateman. Tot est £410. "A house and barn wch Stephen Covell claims to be his own estate."
[Killingly VR: no death record]

[465-467] 17 Mar 1733 will of John Kingsly of Windham "weak in body." Wife Elizabeth Kingsly; son John Kingsly gun and sword; sons Josiah Kingsly and Amos Kingsly; son Ezra Kingsly carpenter tools; dau Tabitha Broughton; to grch, ch of my dau Sarah Hix decd; dau Elizabeth Kingsly may live in house so long as she is single; dau Lydia Kingsly; wife sole exec. Wit: Eleazer Cary, John Abbe, Gershom Palmer. 3 Apr 1733 Windham Capt Eleazer Cary et al. wit oath before Richard Abbe JP. 10 Apr 1733 will exh and ord rec. 7 Jun 1733 rec.
[Windham VR:1:15 John Kinglsey d. 17 Mar 1732/3 ae about 68 years]

[468] 1 Sep 1732 inv. of Elizabeth Parke wid and relict of Isaac Parke decd tken by John Crery, Jona[than] Dean.. Tot est £12. 7 Jun 1733 rec. 12 Apr 1737 Plainfield addition.

[469-470] 10 Apr 1733 distr of estate of Archibald McDowell insolvent by John Crery, William Marsh Jr, Robert Dixon. 7 Jun 1733 rec.

[471-473] 10 Mar 1733 will of Caleb Chappel of Lebanon "sick and weak in body." Wife Ruth; debt to Mr Hubbard and Mr Lowering of Boston; son Joshua; negro man Peter to wife; son Jonathan; son Caleb; negro man Peter to son Jonathan if he outlives my wife; land to son Noah and his male heirs so that it may remain in the name Chappel forever; s-i-l John Strong; s-i-l Samll Gillet; daus Mary, Abijah, Deborah.; son Caleb sole exec. Wit: Aaron Clark, John Williams, Susannah

Windham (Conn.) Probate Records, Vol 1, Sect.1 (1719-1734)

Clark. Testator signs. 9 Apr 1733 Lebanon with oath before Ebenezer West JP; 10 Apr 1733 will exh and ord rec; 8 Jun 1733 rec.
[Lebanon VR:1:46 Lt Caleb Chappell d. 29 Mar 1733]

[474-475] 9 Apr 1733 Lebanon inv of Caleb Chappel decd of Lebanon taken by Stephen Strong, Aaron Clark, Thomas Loomis. Incl Bible, books, pistol, "Peter Negro man £30" Tot est £340. 9 Jun 1733 rec.

[476-478] will of Thomas Huntington of Mansfield "sick and weak in body." Sons Thomas, Jedidiah, Eleazer, William, Simon; daus Elizabeth Hunt and Ruth Lincoln; dau Lydia Huntington for keeping him in "my long lingering sickness;" Thomas gets double portion. Execs: sons Thomas and Jedidiah. Wit: Richard Abbe, James Cross, John Hovey, Joshua Abbe. Testator signs. 13 Dec 1732 wit oath for Capt Thomas Huntington; 13 May 1733 will exh and ord rec. 18 Jun 1733 rec.
[Mansfield VR (Dimmock, 329): Capt Thomas Huntington Esq d. 7 Nov 1732]

[479-480] 3 May 1733 will of Thomas Gallup of Plainfield "sick and weak in body." Nephew Thomas Gallup son of Nathaniel Gallup of Stonington land in Plainfield partly received from my father (mentions Country Road); brothers and sister: John, Samuel, Nathaniel Gallup and Martha Gifford; b-i-l Francis Smith; b-i-l John Smith and two sisters-in-law Sarah Dean and Abijah French; to Pege Douglas "maid with me now;"deceased wife's relations;" bro Nathaniel of Stonington and kinsman John Crery exec. Wit: James Dean Jr, John Douglas, Christabell "H" Harris. 12 Jun 1733 Plainfield wit oath before Timothy Pierce, Asst. ditto will exh and ord rec. 18 Jun 1733 rec.
[Plainfield VR: no death record]

Windham (Conn.) Probate Records, Vol 1, Sect.1 (1719-1734)

[481] 4,5,6 Apr 1733 inv of Mr Samuel Pain of Pomfret decd taken by Joseph Chandler, John Williams, Jacob Dana. Tot est: £2950. 18 Jun 1833 rec. 10 Sep 1734 add £35. [Pomfret VR:1:27 Samuel Paine d. 15 Feb 1732/3]

[482-485] 28,29,30 Apr 1731 inv of Mr Benjamin Phelps of Mansfield decd taken by Deacon Exp[erience] Porter, Samll Gurley, Robert Barrows. Incl gun, powder horn, powder, a staff, a rapier and belt, Bible and books. Tot est £1000. 10 Aug 1733 rec.
[Mansfield VR (Dimmock, 335) Benjamin Phelps d. 18 Apr 1731]

[485] 23 Feb 1729/30 Thomas Wheeler of Plainfield ack from from my bro Benjamin Wheeler of Plainfield £40 from my father Ephraim Wheeler's will. With Timo Pierce, Phoebe Pierce. 7 Sep 1733 rec.

[486] 12 Jun 1733 Elijah Dean and Abigail his wife of Plainfield ack rcpt of Jabez Cary of Preston £14. Cary was gdn for Abigail. Wit: Jo[nathan] Huntington, Solomon Tracy. 6 Sep 1733 rec.

[486] 12 Jun 1733 Jacob Warren of Plainfield now gdn for Zerviah Cary and Hannah Cary ack rcpt from Jabez Carey. Wit; Jo[nathan] Huntington, Solomon Tracy.

[487] 4 Jan 1727 heirs of our father Joseph Cary of Windham decd ack rcpt from mother Marcy Cary, John Cary and Seth Cary. Sign: Nathaniel Skiff, Jabez Cary, Seth Palmer.

[487-488] 7 Aug 1732 Thomas Rugg of Mansfield decd insolvent. Creditors: Deacon Isaac Kendall of Ashford; Theophilus Hall of Mansfield; Stephen Brown for two trips to

Windham (Conn.) Probate Records, Vol 1, Sect.1 (1719-1734)

Lexington [Mass] by order of his father Rugg; Jonathan Rugg of Lexington; Joseph Fassit of Lexington; Joseph Green for making a coffin; Wade Cross for funeral charges; Deacon Conant for rum and sugar; Capt Thomas Storrs for writing the proclamations. 5 Feb 1732/3 done.

[487-491] 1 Mar 1732/3 Court ordered distribution of est of Mr John How of Plainfield decd which we did 10,12,13 Mar 1732/3. Widow Phoebe How, Josiah How eldest son; John How 2^{hd} son; Samuel How 3rd son; James How 4th son; Jonas How 5th son; Lucy How dau. Distr by Daniel Lawrence, Edward Spaulding, Ephraim Kingsbury. 10 May 1733 dist accepted and ord to be recorded.

Windham (Conn.) Probate Records, Vol 1, Sect.2 (1719-1734)

[1] 27 Jun 1733 Mr Thomas Porter of Coventry appt gdn to Josiah Badcock minor son to John Badcock of Windham decd.

[1] 27 Jun 1733 Mr Thomas Porter of Coventry appt gdn to John Badcock minor son to John Badcock of Windham decd.

[1] 27 Jun 1733 Mr Thomas Porter of Coventry appt gdn to Martha Badcock minor dau to John Badcock of Windham decd.

[2] 27 Jun 1733 Mr Josiah Dewey Jr of Lebanon appt gdn to Robert, Hannah, Experience, and John Stedman minor sons and dau to Mr John Stedman decd.

[2] 27 Jun 1733 Mr Peter Scott of Coventry appt gdn to Ichabod Scott minor son to Mr Benjamin Scott of Windham decd.

[3] 13 Mar 1733 Mrs Margaret Griffin relict to Mr Joseph Griffin of Pomfret decd appt gdn to Sarah Griffin minor dau of sd decd. Margaret Griffin is principal gdn and Capt Leicester Grosvenor and Mr Benjamin Griffin sureties.

[3-4] ditto for Joseph, Samuel, and Mary Griffin sons and dau.

[5] 1 Mar 1732/3 Mr Samll Spaulding appt gdn to James How minor son of Mr John How late of Plainfield decd.

[5] 13 Mar 1733 Mr Stephen Brown of Windham appt gdn to Jacob Watrous minor son of Isaac Watrous of Lexington [Mass]

[6] 13 Mar 1733 Mr James Darbie of Canterbury appt gdn to Luce Shephard minor dau to Mr Saml Shephard of Plainfield decd.

Windham (Conn.) Probate Records, Vol 1, Sect.2 (1719-1734)

[6] 13 Mar 1733 Mr Leicester Grosvenor appt gdn to Ebenezer Grosvenor minor son of Ebenezer Grosvenor of Pomfret decd.

[7] ditto for minor son Caleb.

[7] 13 Mar 1733 Mr William Durkee of Windham appt gdn to Henry Durkee a minor son of Mr William Durkee of Windham decd.

[8] ditto for minor dau Hannah.

[8] 13 Mar 1733 Mrs Elizabeth Kingsley relict to John Kingsley of Windham decd appt gdn to Lydia Kingsley minor dau of sd decd.

[9] 4 Apr 1733 Mr Joseph Levengs Esq of Killingly appt gdn to James Levings minor son of Mr Benjamin Levings of Killingly decd.

[9] 21 Sep 1732 Mr Joseph Lawrence of Plainfield appt gdn to Benoni Thomson minor son of Mr Peter Thomson of Rantom, Mass. [Wrentham?]

[10] 7 Dec 1732 Mr Daniel Church of Killingly appt gdn to Jonathan Church minor son of Mr Samll Church decd.

[10] 12 Jan 1733 Mr Joshua Chappell of Lebanon appt gdn to Jabez Chappell minor son of Mr Caleb Chappell of Lebanon decd.

[11] 12 Jun 1733 Mr Jacob Warren of Plainfield appt gdn to Zurviah Cary minor dau of Mr Joseph Cary of Windham decd.

Windham (Conn.) Probate Records, Vol 1, Sect.2 (1719-1734)

[11] ditto minor dau Hannah

[12] [blank page]

[13] 14 Nov 1732 Archibald McDowell insolvent estate.

[14] [blank page]

[15] 9 Jan 1732/3 admin of est of Mr Ebenezer Hibbard of Windham decd req support for Shubael Hibbard minor son of sd decd. Granted £12.

[16] 9 Jan 1732/3 Mr Jonathan Clough of Killingly appt gdn to David Cutting minor son of Mr David Cutting of Killingly decd.

[17] 28 Jun 1732 Mr Jedediah Phelps of Lebanon appt gdn to Benjamin Phelps minor son of Mr Benjamin Phelps of Mansfield decd.

[17] 14 Nov 1732 Mr Joseph Done admin of William Hamlet decd pd Mr Ebenezer Holbrook, gdn.

[18] 27 Jun 1732 Mr John Fuller of Mansfield appt gdn to Abigail Phelps minor dau of Mr Benjamin Phelps of Mansfield decd.

[18] ditto for minor dau Ann.

[19] ditto Mr Joseph Davis of Mansfield for minor dau Martha.

[19] 6 Jan 1737/8 Mr Samuel Butler of Wilmington, Mass. appt gdn to William Hamlet minor son of Mr William Hamlet of Pomfret decd.

Windham (Conn.) Probate Records, Vol 1, Sect. 2 (1719-1734)

[20] 25 Jan 1730/1 Joshua Preston of Killingly minor son of Samuel Preston of Andover [Mass or Conn?] chose Mr Levi Preston of Killingly as gdn.

[20] 6 Jan 1737/8 Mr Joseph Hamblett of Nottingham, Mass appt gdn to Rebecca Hamlett minor dau of Mr William Hamlett of Pomfret decd.

[21] 14 Mar 1732 Archibald McDowell of Norwich decd. William McDowell is admin.

[22] 6 Jun 1732 Mr Jabez Dillino [i.e. Delano] of Tolland appt gdn to Reuben Hibbard minor son of Mr Ebenezer Hibbard of Windham decd. Ditto for minor dau Abigail.

[23] 7 Aug 1732 Mr John Carbour/Carbrough/Scarbrough of Woodstock and Dorothy his wife admins of Mr Nathan Right of Ashford. Set out to widow.

[24] 8 Feb 1731/2 ditto. Request more time.

[24] 11 Nov 1735 ditto. Quietus est granted.

[24] 22 Aug 1730 Benjamin Leavings minor son of Mr Benjamin Levings of Killingly decd chose Mr Joseph Levings Esq as gdn.

[25] 12 Oct 1731 Malatiah Conant minor son of Caleb Conant of Mansfield decd chose Mr Josiah Conant of Mansfield as gdn.

[25] 25 Jun 1734 Mr Josiah Conant of Mansfield Esq appt gdn to Benajah Conant minor son of Mr Caleb Conant of Windham decd.

Windham (Conn.) Probate Records, Vol 1,Sect.2 (1719-1734)

[26] 11 Jan 1731/2 Naomi Lovejoy minor dau of John Lovejoy of Plainfield decd chose Mr Ephraim Spaulding of Plainfield as gdn.

[27] 11 Jan 1731/2 Mr Mark Williams of Preston appt gdn to Huldah Frost minor dau of Mr Stephen Frost of Canterbury decd.

[28] 22 Dec 1731 Mr Isaac Limond [i.e. Lyman] of Lebanon with his wife Rebecca appt gdn to Rachel Ardua [Ardona?], Mary and Sarah minor daus of Mr Jacob Ardua of Pomfret decd.

[28] 22 Dec 1731 Mr Nathaniel Holbrook of Lebanon appt gdn to Daniel and John Ardua minor sons of Mr Jacob Ardua of Pomfret decd.

[29] 9 Nov 1731 Mr Joseph Hamlit of Dunstable, Mass appt gdn to Rebecca Hamlit minor dau of Mr William Hamlett of Pomfret decd.

[29] 9 Nov 1731 Mr Ebenezer Holbrook of Pomfret appt gdn to William Hamlit minor son of Mr William Hamlett of Pomfret decd.

[30] 20 Dec 1731 Mr Israel Fullsomar of Windham appt gdn to John Mason minor son of Robert Mason of Ashford decd.

[31] 16 Dec 1731 Mr Jonathan Bingham of Windham appt gdn to Jonathan Mason minor son of Mr Hez[ekiah] Mason of Windham decd.

Windham (Conn.) Probate Records, Vol 1,Sect.2 (1719-1734)

[31] 16 Dec 1731 Mr Elkanah Fuller of Mansfield appt gdn to Judeah Fuller minor son of Mr Samuel Fuller of Mansfield decd.

[32] 16 Dec 1731 Thankful Luce minor dau of Mr Israel Luce of Windham decd chose Mr Joshua Wite [i.e. White] of Windham gdn.

[32] 16 Dec 1731 Mr John Bass of Windham appt gdn to Mary Luce minor dau of Mr Israel Luce of Windham decd.

[33] 15 Dec 1731 Mr Benjamin Follit of Windham appt gdn to Israel Dimmock and Ebenezer Dimmock minor sons of Mr Timothy Dimmock of Ashford decd.

[34] 23 Jun 1731 Hubart Estabrooks minor son of Rev. Mr Samll Estabrooks of Canterbury decd chose Rev. Mr Ebenezer [i.e. Eleazer] Williams of Mansfield as gdn.

[35] 28 Mar 1728 Joseph Preston Jr of Windham minor son of Joseph Preston of Andover, Mass, decd chose his father-in-law Mr Robert Holt of Windham, gdn.

[35] 31 Mar 1731 Nathaniel Luce minor son of Josiah Luce of Windham, decd chose Mr Joshua Lasel of Windham gdn.

[36] 8 Jun 1731 Josiah How minor son of Mr John How of Plainfield decd chose his mother Mrs Phoebe How gdn.

[36] 10 Aug 1731 Martha Smith minor dau of Mr Elisha Smith of Windham chose Mr Ebenezer Wales of Windham gdn.

Windham (Conn.) Probate Records, Vol 1,Sect.2 (1719-1734)

[37] 9 Jul 1729 James Pike and Jonathan Pike minor sons of John Pike of Canterbury decd chose John Pike of Canterbury gdn.

[37] 19 Dec 1730 Zebediah Scott minor son of Benjamin Scott of Windham decd chose Peter Scott of Windham gdn.

[38] 7 Dec 1730 Timothy Grover and Jonathan Grover both aged 14 chose Deacon Eleazer Bateman gdn.

[39] [blank page]

[40] 14 Jul 1730 Mr Jonathan Silsby appt gdn to Bethia Lile dau to Mr George Lilie of Windham decd.

[41] 10 Mar 1719/20 Court appts Jacob Lillie adm for est of George Lillie of Windham decd. Bondsmen: Mr Samuel Palmer, Jonathan Silsby.

[41] 20 Mar 1719/20 Will of John Hutchison of Lebanon decd exh by widow and son John Hutchison execs, and ord rec.

[41] 18 Feb 1719/20 Will of Ebenezer Brown of Canterbury decd exh by his son Deliverance Brown exec and ord rec.

[42] 23 Mar 1720 Letters of adm for est of William Douglas of Plainfield decd granted to John Deane of Groton. Bondsmen: Mr Thomas Thatcher and Rhodolphus Thatcher.

[42] 5 Aug 1720 Will of Thomas Kingsberrie of Plainfield decd exh by Sarah Kingsberrie exec widow of sd Thomas Kingsberrie

Windham (Conn.) Probate Records, Vol 1, Sect.2 (1719-1734)

[42] Inv of William Douglas of Plainfield decd exh by John Dean.

[43] 4 Apr 1720 Ebenezer Fitch of Windsor on behalf of his wife Bridgit; Ebenezer Brown of Concord [Mass]; Thomas Brown of Canterbury; Ebenezer Davice of Concord [Mass] appeal to Superior Court 31 Aug 1720 appeal withdrawn.

[43] 15 Jul 1720 Letters of adm on est of Joseph Blackman granted to Elizabeth Blackman widow and to son Elisha Blackman and to Jonathan Medcalf. Bondsman: Mr Simon Newcombe. Inv of Joseph Blackman exh and ord rec.

[44] 15 Jul 1720 John Dean appt gdn to Mary Douglace she desiring the same.

[44] 10 Jan 1720/1 Will of Joseph Parkhurst of Plainfield decd exh by his widow and son John Parkhurst. Inv exh and ord rec.

[44] 10 Jan 1720/1 Timothy Parkhurst appt gdn to Samuel Parkhurst he desiring same.

[44] 4 Dec 1722 Samuel Parkman ack rcpt from Timothy Parkhurst.

[45] 7 Mar 1720 Letters of adm on est of Joseph Wilson of Ashford decd granted to Jacob Parker and Mary Wilson. Bondsmen: Isaac Kindal and Joshua Kindal. 4 Feb 1743/4 quietus est granted. Inv exh and ord rec.

[46] 7 Mar 1720 Simon Newcomb appt gdn to Caleb Jones he desiring same.

Windham (Conn.) Probate Records, Vol 1, Sect. 2 (1719-1734)

[46] 7 Mar 1720 Joseph Cary appt gdn to Lidea Lillie she desiring same.

[46] 7 Mar 1720 Jonathan Silsby appt gdn to Bethia Lillie she desiring same.

[46] 7 Mar 1720 Jacob Lillie appt gdn to Reuben and Sarah Lillie they desiring same.

[47] 15 Mar 1721 Jacob Lillie adm of est of George Lillie. Tot: £460.10.0. Distr: Jacob Lillie eldest son; Elisha Lillie; Reuben Lillie; Elizabeth Lillie; Mary Lillie, Sarah Lillie; Lydia Lillie; Bethiah Lillie. Land to be distr by Mr Samuel Palmer, Samuel Webb, Jonathan Silsbie. Quietus est granted.

[48] 4 Jul 1721 Letters of adm granted on est of Benjamin Smalley of Lebanon decd unto Rebeckah Smalley. Bondsman: Nathan Tuttle and Caleb Lummas. 6 Nov 1722 inv exh and ord rec.

[49] 4 Jul 1722 Letter of admin granted on est of George Webster of Lebanon decd to Sarah Webster. Bondsmen: John Sprague and John Woodward. Inv exh and ord rec.

[49] 4 Jul 1722 Jonathan Silsbie appt gdn to Liddiah Lillie she desiring same.

[50] 13 Feb 1721/2 Letters of adm granted on est of Deacon Joseph Cary of Windham decd to Mercy Cary, John Cary and Seth Cary. Bondsmen: Jonathan Crane and Ralph Whelock. Inv exh and ord rec. 4 Apr 1723 quietus est granted.

[51] 6 Apr 1722 Letter of admin granted on est of Joseph Cary Jr of Windham decd to Abigail Cary. Bondsmen: Joseph

Windham (Conn.) Probate Records, Vol 1,Sect.2 (1719-1734)

Bushnell, Nathan Bushnell. Inv exh and ord rec. 6 Nov 1722 quietus est granted.

[51] 6 Apr 1722 Inv of est of Joseph Cary Jr of Windham decd exh by Abigail Cary and ord rec.

[51] 6 Apr 1722 Rebeckah Smalley of Lebanon quietus est granted as admin of est of Benjamin Smalley of Lebanon decd.

[52] 6 Nov 1722 Rebeckah Smalley adm of Benjamin Smalley of Lebanon decd presented acct of adm. Total: £440.11.10. Hannah Clark already received £9; Rebeckah Woodworth already received £2.16.0. Court orders remainder distr: to widow Rebeckah Smalley; eldest son Benjamin Smalley; James Smalley; Joseph Smalley, and Frances Smalley. Land to sons. Henry Woodward and Josiah Lyman of Lebanon appt to distribute estate.

[53] 29 Jan 1722/3 Will of William Shaw of Windham decd exh by widow exec. Inv also.

[53] 13 Feb 1722/3 Letters of adm on est of Isaac Hill of Pomfret decd granted to Sarah Hill. Bond: Eliezur Bateman and Jacob Wright.

[54] 5 Mar 1722/3 Letters of admin on est of Capt Thomas Williams decd granted to Thomas Williams of Plainfield son of decd. Bond: Jacob Warrin and John Hall. 12 Jan 1725/6 Thomas Williams pd debts.

[55] 5 Apr 1723 Will of John Waldin of Windham decd exh by his son John Waldin exec. Inv exh and ord rec.

Windham (Conn.) Probate Records, Vol 1,Sect.2 (1719-1734)

[55] 5 Apr 1723 Will of William Price of Ashford decd exh by his wife Sarah Price exec. Inv exh and ord rec.

[56-57] 4 Apr 1723 Henry Cary, Joseph Cary, Seth Cary all of Windham adm of est of Deacon Joseph Cary of Windham decd present acct of admin. Tot: £362.13.0. Mercy Cary widow; eldest son double portion; Jabez Cary, John Cary, Seth Cary; Nathaniel Skiff in right of his wife Hannah "his father Cary;" Seth Palmer in right of his wife; eldest son is deceased. Court appts Capt Eliezur Cary, Mr Jonah Palmer and Mr Ralph Wheelock of Windham as distributors.

[57-58] 3 May 1723 Abigail Warrin widow of Joseph Cary of Windham decd and admin of same presents acct of admin. Tot: £222.7.0. Court distr: to Abigail Warren, to Abigail Cary, to Zerviah Cary, to Hannah Cary. Court appts Ens. Nathaniel Rudd and Sgt Samuel Bingham to distribute est. 3 May 1723 Quietus est granted.

[58] 3 May 1723 Will of Nathaniel Skiff of Windham decd exh by his son Nathaniel Skiff exec. Inv also exh.

[58] 21 Dec 1739 Quietus est granted on est of Dr Isaac Hill of Pomfret decd.

[59] [undated] Abigail Warrin of Plainfield late widow of Joseph Cary of Windham decd appt gdn to Abigail Cary, Zerviah Cary, and Hannah Cary daus of sd decd. Bond: Jacob Warrin and Abigail Warrin.

[59] 30 Apr 1723 Jabez Cary appeals distr of est of his father Joseph Cary of Windham decd. Homestead was distr to youngest son Seth Cary instead of eldest son (sd Jabez Cary). Court allows appeal to Superior Court. Bond: William Allin and John Flint both of Windham.

Windham (Conn.) Probate Records, Vol 1,Sect.2 (1719-1734)

[60] 1 Oct 1723 Letters of adm on est of John Ensworth of Plainfield decd granted to Elizabeth Ensworth. Bond: Joseph Cleveland and Joseph Ainsworth. Inv exh. 8 Nov 1726 Mrs Elizabeth Ensworth admin presents an account.

[61] 10 Dec 1723 Will of William Ballard of Plainfield decd exh by execs Enoch and Peleg Ballard. Inv also.

[61] 11 Nov 1735 Mrs Elizabeth Ensworth widow of Mr John Ensworth of Canterbury decd since married to Mr Christopher Huntington of Norwich and is since decd. Mr Joseph Cleveland is now admin and granted quietus est. 14 Apr 1741 quietus est granted on est of John Ensworth decd.

[62] 14 Jan 1723/4 Letters of adm on est of Simon Orne of Providence decd on est in Windham. Court appts Humphrey Ballard to make inv. Bond: John Broughton of Windham and Gershom Clarke of Lebanon.

[63] 24 Apr 1724 Letters of adm on est of Elizabeth Harris late of New London relict of Peter Harris of New London decd on land in Mansfield granted to Samuel Harris of New London. Bond: Mr Samuel Huntington and Mr Timothy Clarke both of Lebanon. Inv exhibited.

[64] 22 Apr 1724 Sarah Webster of Lebanon exec of George Webster of Lebanon decd reports £1096.09.09. Court distr: wife Sarah Webster; Samuel Webster eld son; Jonathan Webster 2nd son; Peletiah Webster 3rd son; George Webster; Noah Webster; Ebenezer Webster; Benajah Webster; Joseph Webster; Abigail Webster; Sarah Webster; Jerusha Webster; Zerviah Webster; and Mary Webster. Court appts Capt Joseph Marsh and Ens. Samuel Huchison of Lebanon to distr est.

Windham (Conn.) Probate Records, Vol 1,Sect.2 (1719-1734)

[65] 22 Apr 1724 Sarah Webster widow of George appt gdn to Benajah and Joseph her sons and Jerusha and Mary her daus, sons and daus of George Webster. Bond: John Webster.

[65] 22 Apr 1724 Samuel Webster of Lebanon eldest son of George Webster appt gdn to George Webster, Noah Webster, Ebenezer Webster, and Sarah Webster and Zerviah Webster sons and daus of George Webster decd. Bond Samuel Webster and Sgt John Webster.

[65] 22 Apr 1724 Mr John Bliss, Mr John Webster, Jedediah Strong appt appraisers. [John Bliss marks "B"]

[66] 11 Aug 1724 Letters of adm on est of Seth Smith of Coventry decd granted to Ebenezer Wales of Windham. Bond: Mr Jonathan Bingham of Windham and Mr Jonathan Metcalf of Lebanon. Inv exh. 23 Jul 1725 admin not ready and delay allowed.

[67] 1 Oct 1725 Letters of adm on est of Benjamin Levins of Killingly decd granted to Elizabeth. Bond: Mr James Levins, Mr Joseph Levins both of Killingly. 29 Sep 1727 Mrs Elizabeth Horsmer adm of est of Benjamin Levins decd presents acct. Tot: £86.10.7.

[68] 4 Dec 1724 Letters of adm on est of of Mr John Hall of Plainfield decd granted to Thomas Stephens Jr of Plainfield. Bond: Mr John Crery, Mr John Parkhurst. Inv exh.

[68] 4 Dec 1724 Letters of adm on est of Ebenezer Crowfut of Lebanon granted to Joanna Crowfut. Bond: _akiniah Loomis of Lebanon and Samuel Crowfut of Springfield [Mass]

Windham (Conn.) Probate Records, Vol 1, Sect.2 (1719-1734)

[69] 29 Dec 1724 Letters of adm on est of Mr Samuel Shepard of Plainfield decd granted to Elinor Shepard widow of sd decd. Bond: Mr Daniel Larence and Mr Joseph Williams both of Plainfield. Inv exh.

[69] 29 Dec 1724 Letters of adm on est of Mr Jonathan Davice of Canterbury granted to Mr Ephraim Davice father to the decd. Bond: Mr Daniel Laurence and Mr Joseph Williams of Plainfield. Inv exh.

[70] 12 Jan 1724/5 will of Samuel How of Plainfield decd exh by exec John How. Inv exh.

[70] 22 Jan 1724/5 will of Jeremiah Durke of Windham exh by his exec Paul Holt. Inv exh.

[70] 22 Jan 1724/5 Letters of adm on est of Mr Thomas Durke of Windham decd granted to William Durke of Windham. Bond: Nathaniel Kingsbury, Thomas Marsh.

[71] 27 Jan 1724/5 Letters of adm on est of Thomas Whiting of Killingly decd granted to John Whiting of Haverill, Mass. Bond: Samson How of Killingly, and Edmond Hovey of Mansfield.

[71] 26 Jan 1724/5 Court provides support for Mrs Elizabeth Blackman relict to Mr Joseph Blackman of Lebanon decd.

[72] 9 Mar 1724/5 Thomas Stevens of Plainfield adm of est of Mr John Hall of Plainfield exh acct.

[72] 9 Mar 1724/5 Thomas Stevens 2nd appt gdn to Uriah Stevens, Fineas Stevens, Andrew Stevens, Benjamin Stevens, Samuel Stevens and Zebulon Stevens his children by Mary his first wife.

Windham (Conn.) Probate Records, Vol 1, Sect. 2 (1719-1734)

[72] 9 Mar 1724/5 John How exec of Mr Samuel How of Plainfield decd exh an account. 22 Nov 1726 same.

[73] 22 Mar 1725 Letters of adm on est of Mr William Hamlett of Pomfret decd to Rebeckah Hamblett widow. Bond: Abial Lyon, Ebenezer Holebrook both Pomfret.

[73] 29 Mar 1725 Will of Mr John Adams of Canterbury decd exh by his widow Michael [sic] Adams and Richaard Adams. Inv exh also.

[73] 10 Apr 1732 Mr Joseph Dene adm of Mr William Hamlit of Pomfret decd presents an acct.

[74] 5 Apr 1725 Letters of adm on est of Mr Phillip Bump of Plainfield decd granted to Phillip Bump, 2nd son to decd. Bond: Mr John Fellows of Plainfield and Samuel Bump of Bolton.

[74] 21 Jun 1725 Letters of adm on est of Samuel Sprague of Lebanon decd granted to Mary Sprague relict to decd and Capt Ephraim Sprague of Lebanon. Bond: Mr John Huchison and John Sprague Jr of Lebanon. Inv exh.

[75] 21 Jun 1725 Letters of adm on est of Jonathan Royce of Lebanon decd granted to Ruth Royce widow and Ens. John Huchison of Lebanon. Bond: John Sprague. Inv exh.

[75] 21 Jun 1725 Letters of adm on est of Capt William Clarke Esq. of Lebanon decd granted to Mrs Mary Clarke and Deacon William Clark eldest son of decd both of Lebanon. Bond: Mr Jonathan Liman, Mr Caleb Pierce of Lebanon. 9 Dec 1725 Inv and distr plan exh and quietus est granted.

Windham (Conn.) Probate Records, Vol 1, Sect.2 (1719-1734)

[76-77 missing]

[78] 29 Jun 1725 Letters of adm on est of Mr Frances Barker [or Parker] of Killingly decd granted to Martha Barker [or Parker] relict to decd. Bond: Mr Jacob Spaulding of Killingly and Mr John Rusel of Plainfield. 7 Apr 1726 Mrs Martha Barker [or Parker] exh acct.

[79] 30 Jun 1725 Will of Mr James Deen of Plainfield decd exh by his sons James Dean and John Dean. Inv exh.

[80] 5 Jul 1725 Letters of adm on est of David Cuting of Killingly decd granted to Elizabeth Cuting relict to decd. Bond: Mr Eleazer Bateman, Mr James Levengs both of Killingly. 11 Apr 1727 Mrs Elizabeth Cutting of Plainfield adm of David Cutting exh acct.

[80] 10 Jan 1743/4 Quietus est granted on est of Joseph Wilson of Ashford.

[81] 13 Jul 1725 Letters of adm on est of Samuel Spaulding of Canterbury decd granted to Mary Spaulding relict to sd decd and to Samuel Spaulding of Pomfret. Bond: John Woodward and Joseph Cleveland. Inv exh. 8 Mar 1725/6 Mr Samuel Spaulding exh acct. 12 Apr 1726 Mrs Mary Spaulding exh acct.

[82] 13 Jul 1725 Letters of adm on est of John Lovejoy of Plainfield decd grantedd to Barthsheba Lovejoy relict. Bond: Ambros Blunt and Timothy Parkhurst. Inv exh. 22 Nov 17226 Mrs Barthsheba Lovejoy exh acct.

[83] 13 Jul 1725 Will of Jonathan Rigbe of Plainfield decd exh by his widow/exec. Bond: John Parkhurst and Samuel

Windham (Conn.) Probate Records, Vol 1,Sect.2 (1719-1734)

Parkhurst for Hannah Rigbe exec. 3 May 1726 Mrs Hannah Rigbe exh acct. 13 Jun 1727 Mrs Hannah Rigbe exh acct.

[84] 13 Jul 1725 Will of Mr Ephraim Wheeler of Plainfield decd exh by his son Benjamin Wheeler exec. Bond: Ephraim Kingsbury, John How. 11 Jun 1725/6 Benjamin Wheeler exh acct.

[84] 11 Jan 1725/6 Samuel Spaulding appt gdn to Thomas Wheeler, he desiring same. Ens. Ephraim Kingsbury appt gdn to Olive Wheeler she desiring same. Lt Edward Spaulding of Canterbury appt gdn of Mary Wheeler. Mr Martow [Martin?] Huntington of Preston appt gdn to Edward Wheeler.

[85] 23 Jul 1725 Letters of adm on est of Robert Willes of Ashford decd granted to Lydia Willes relict to sd decd. Bond: Nathaniel Kingsbury and Richard Abbe. Inv exh.

[85] 12 Aug 1735 adm of Robert Willes of Ashford decd exh acct.

[86] 14 Sep 1731 Mr William Rusill husband to the widow and relict of Mr John Chapman of Ashford decd exh acct. 8 Jun 1736 Quietus est granted.

[86] 24 Feb 1725/6 Mr Phillip Bump adm of Mr Phillip Bump of Plainfield decd exh an agreement. Quietus est granted.

[87] 23 Jul 1725 Letters of adm on est of James Richardson of Windham decd granted to Mary Richardson. Bond: Mr Nathaniel Kingsbury and Richard Abbe. Inv exh.

Windham (Conn.) Probate Records, Vol 1, Sect.2 (1719-1734)

[88] 23 Jul 1725 Will of Mr Nathaniel Hebbard of Windham decd exh by widow exec. Inv exh. Bond: Mr Jonathan Crane to Sarah Hibard exec.

[89] 23 Jul 1725 Letters of adm on est of Robert Simons of Windham decd granted to Jacob Simons son of decd. Bond: Richard Abbe.

[90] 14 Sep 1725 Letters of adm on est of Mr Edward Spaulding of Plainfield decd granted to Dorithy Spaulding late wife to decd. Bond: Mr John How and John Crery. Inv exh. 29 Sep 1728 Dorothy Spaulding exh acct. 29 Sep 1728 Dorothy Spaulding appt gdn to her son Jacob Spaulding.

[91] 5 Sep 1725 Letters of adm on est of Mr John Burnap of Windham decd granted to Mr Isaac Burnap of sd Windham. Bond: Deacon Joshua Whitney and Mr Henry Adams. Inv exh.

[91] 14 Aug 1739 Dorothy Spaulding granted Quietus est.

[92] 9 Nov 1725 Letters of adm on est of Mr Benjamin Palmour of Plainfield decd granted to Mr Joseph Lawrence. Bond: Thomas Stevens. Inv. exh. 11 Jul 1727 Joseph Lawrence exh agreement and Quietus est granted.

[93] 9 Nov 1725 Letters of adm on est of Rev Mr Samuel Whiting of Windham decd granted to Elizabeth Whiting widow. Bond: Mr Joseph Fitch of Lebanon and Mr Joseph Bradford of New London. Inv exh. 13 Sep 1726 Rev Samuel Whiting estate total: £455.10.1.

[94] [blank page]

Windham (Conn.) Probate Records, Vol 1, Sect.2 (1719-1734)

[95-96] Mrs Mary Spaulding and Samuel Spaulding of Canterbury adm of Lt Samuel Spaulding of Canterbury decd estate total £841.9.5. Court orders distr: Mrs Mary Spaulding; Samuel Spaulding eldest son; Jonas Spaulding 2nd son; Zachariah Spaulding 3rd; Jonathan Spaulding 4th; Mary Spaulding eldest dau; Bridgit Spaulding 2nd dau. Court appts Mr Elisha Pain and Deac Thomas Brown and Mr Daniel Cady of Canterbury to distribute the est. Court appts Mr John Woodward of Canterbury gdn to Mary Spaulding she desiring same. Court appts Mr Joseph Cleveland of Canterbury gdn to Jonathan Spaulding son of Lt Spaulding decd and also to Bridgit Spaulding youngest dau of sd decd.

[96] 3 May 1726 Mrs Elinor Shepard adm of est of Mr Samuel Shepard of Plainfield decd exh acct.

[97] 6 Jun 1726 Mr John Whiting adm of est of Mr Thomas Whiting of Killingly decd exh acct.

[97] 15 Mar 1727 Mrs Mary Spaulding, Samuel Spaulding, Jonas Spaulding, John Woodward, Joseph Cleveland, Zachariah Spaulding req to have other gentlemen distr est they being dissatisfied with the distr done. Ct grants req and appts Capt Joseph Adams, Mr Benjamin Fassit and Mr Nathaniel Robins of Canterbury.

[98] 1 Aug 1726 Letters of adm on est of Mr Joseph Woodward of Canterbury decd granted to Mrs Hannah Woodward widow of decd. Bond: Mr Stephen Frost. Inv exh.

[99] 14 Sep 1726 Petition of Edward Spaulding and John Smith on behalf of their wives as heirs to the est of Lt John Hall decd and Thomas Stevens Jr adm of est desire distr. Court denies req but allows appeal to Superior Court. John

Windham (Conn.) Probate Records, Vol 1,Sect.2 (1719-1734)

Smith is of Voluntown; Edward Spaulding and Thomas Stevens Jr are of Plainfield.

[100] 13 Sep 1726 Will of Mr John Mory of Lebanon decd exh by his adm. 18 Jun 1733 Mr Joseph Marton adm exh acct.

[101] 13 Sep 1726 Will of Benjamin Franklin of Pomfret decd exh by Mr Thomas Bettes exec.

[102-103] 10 Nov 1726 Mrs Elinor Shepard adm of Mr Samuel Shepard of Plainfield decd total estate £1096.7.7. Court distr: Mrs Elinor Shepard widow; Jonathan Shepard eldest son; David Shepard 2nd son; Nathan Shepard 3rd son; Benjamin Shepard 4th son; Eleanor Darbyshr wife to James Darbyshr eld dau of decd; Mary Jonson wife to James Jonson 2nd dau; Luce Shephard 3rd dau. Court appts: Deacon Jacob Warin, Mr Ephraim Kingsbury and Mr Daniel Lawrance of Plainfield to distr est. Court appts Deacon Joshua Whitney gdn to Jonathan and David Shepard they desiring the same. Court appts Mr David Whitney gdn to Nathan and Benjamin and Lucy Shepard sons and dau of decd. 21 Dec 1730 Jacob Jonson of Canterbury re est of Mr Samuel Shepard of Plainfield decd.

[104] 8 Nov 1726 Will of Mr Jonathan Hides of Canterbury decd exh by Mr Jonathan Hides of Pomfret exec. Bond: Mr James Hides.

[105] 8 Nov 1726 Letters of adm on est of Mr James Leach of Windham decd granted to Mrs Mary Leach widow to sd decd. Bond: Mr Thomas Durke and Mr Clement Neff. Inv exh. 13 Jun 1727 Mrs Mary Leach exh acct.

Windham (Conn.) Probate Records, Vol 1, Sect.2 (1719-1734)

[106] 22 Nov 1726 Letters of adm on est of Mr James Welch of Plainfield decd granted to James Welch eldest son of sd decd. Bond: Mr Benjamin Clark and Ebenezer Welch. Inv exh. 18 Jun 1728 Quietus est granted to Mr James Welch adm.

[107] 14 Dec 1726 Mrs Ebenezer Walles adm to est of Seth Smith of Coventry decd estate total: £122.11.0. The Real Estate of sd Deceased being his own estate and Not Descended from his Father. Therefor This Court settles ye Whool of ye sd Real Estate of ye sd Deceased on his only sister Estar Walles wife to sd Ebenezer Walles. She being "ye Whool blood only." Personal est to same and also to Martha Smith half sister of decd. Court appts Mr Jonathan Bingham and Mr Joseph Bingham and Mr Jabez Huntington to distr est.

[108] 19 Dec 1726 Letters of adm on est of Mr Jacob Ardeway of Moltlack [i.e. Mortlake] decd to Mr Abel Right of Windham and Mrs Rebeca Ardaway of Moltlack. Bond: Ebenezer Wright, Ephram Wright. 15 Dec 1727 Abel Right exh inv.

[109] 13 Dec 1726 Will of Mr Samuel Throop of Lebanon decd exh by Mr Dan Throop exec. Bond: Mr Benjamin Seabury and Mr Joseph Fowler.

[110] 26 Jan 1726/7 Letters of adm on est of Mr Josiah Backar [i.e. Baker] of Lebanon decd granted to George Partridg of Duxbury [Mass]. Bond: Mr Joshua Eells of Lebanon.

[111] 16 Dec 1726 Mr Jacob Simons adm of est of Mr Robert Simons of Windham decd exh acct: £51.19.6. Court distr: Mrs Tamson Simons relict to decd; heirs of Mr Robert Simons of Windham decd eldest son; Mr Jonathan Simons; Mr

Windham (Conn.) Probate Records, Vol 1, Sect.2 (1719-1734)

David Simons; Jacob Simons; Ebenezer Simons. Court appts: Mr Benjamin Scott, Mr Jeremiah Ripley, Mr Benjamin Follet to distr est.

[112] 29 Mar 1727 Thomas Stevens adm of est of Lt John Hall upon act of Superior Court held 25 Mar 1727. Tot inv: £1307.11.4. Court distr: Mr Samuel Hall of Stoo [i.e. Stow, Mass] eld bro of decd; Mr Stephen Hall of Charlestown [Mass.} 2nd bro of decd; heirs of Ruth Stevens eld sister to decd; Susannah Smith 2nd sis of decd; to heirs of Mary Stevens 3rd sis to decd. Elizabeth Spaulding 4th sis of decd; Sarah Bloggit youngest sister of decd. Court appts Mr Daniel Lawrance, Mr Joseph Williams of Plainfield and Mrs Thomas Roas of Preston to divide estate. Court appts Mr Thomas Stevens 2nd gdn to Uriah Stevens and Andru Stevens sons of sd Mary Stevens they desiring same; also appts sd Thomas Stevens gdn to Benjamin Stevens, Samuel Stevens, and Zebulon Stevens sons of sd Mary Stevens.

[113] 29 Mar 1727 Mr Thomas Stevens 2nd gdn to Uriah Stevens, Andru Stevens, Benjamin Stevens, Samuel Stevens and Zebulon Stevens sons to Mary Stevens first wife of sd Thomas Stevens, posts bond.

[113] 5 Apr 1727 Mr John Smith of Voluntown posts bond on est of Lt John Hall of Plainfield decd.

[113] 5 Apr 1727 Mr Edward Spaulding posts bond on ditto.

[113] 5 Apr 1727 Thomas Stevens 2nd of Plainfield ditto.

[113] 5 Apr 1727 Mr John Stevens posts bond for himself and the rest of his bros and sisters ditto.

Windham (Conn.) Probate Records, Vol 1, Sect.2 (1719-1734)

[113] 5 Apr 1727 Court grantes Quietus est on est of Lt John Hall to Thomas Stevens Jr.

[114] 7 Mar 1726/7 Letters on est of Mr Stephen Lee of Lebanon decd granted to Elezebeth Lee widow of sd decd. Bond: Samuel Lee, John Gillit. Inv exh.

[114] 25 Feb 1735/6 Quietus est granted to Mrs Elizabeth Lee adm of est of Mr Stephen Lee of Lebanon decd.

[115] 7 Mar 1726/7 Letters of adm on est of Mr Samuel Stetson of Mansfield decd granted to Capt Thomas Storrs, Ebenezer Dunham, Desiah Stetson. Bond: John Dunham, Barnabus Hall.

[115] 18 Decc 1731 Mr Ebenezer Dunham exh acct.

[116] 6 Mar 1726/7 Letters of adm on est of Josiah Luce of Windham decd granted to Mr John Cary and Sarah Luce. Bond: Nathaniel Rudd, Joseph Waldon. Inv exh.

[116] 12 Sep 1733, 11 Mar 1735, 13 Jan 1736/7, 14 Feb 1737/8 adm of est of Mr Josiah Luce exh acct [mentions raising younger children]

[117] 6 Mar 1726/7 Will of Mr Thomas Cushman of Lebanon decd exh by execs.

[117] 9 Feb 1737/8 Quietus est granted on estate of Mr Josiah Luce of Windham decd.

[118] 11 Apr 1727 Letters of adm on est of Mr Thomas Fanning of Stonington decd granted to Timothy [Nanpolt?] and the widow to sd decd. Bond: Timothy [Nanpolt?] and Nathaniel Ayr.

Windham (Conn.) Probate Records, Vol 1, Sect.2 (1719-1734)

[119-120] 11 Apr 1727 Mr Richard Abbe and Mrs Elezebeth Whiting adm of est of Rev Mr Samuel Whiting of Windham decd. Total inv: £1249.3.1. William Whiting is eldest son. Land in Hebron mentioned. Mr Joseph Fitch husband to eld dau; Mr John Backus Jr huband of Sybbel 3rd dau. Court distr: Mrs Elezebeth Whiting widow to sd decd; Joseph Fitch husb of An [i.e. Ann] eld dau of decd; Mr John Backus husb of Sibbel 3rd dau of decd; Mary Whiting 4th dau; John Whiting 2nd son to sd decd; Eliphalet Whiting 3rd son; Elisha Whiting 4th son; Samuel Whiting 5th son; Joseph Whiting 6th son; Nathan Whiting youngest son. Court appts Capt John Fitch, Mr Samuel Webb and Lt Jeremiah Ripley all of Windham to divide est.

[121] 20 Apr 1727 Mrs Elezebeth Whiting relict to Rev Mr Samuel Whiting of Windham decd appt gdn to Mary Mary Whiting 4th dau she desiring the same; also appt gdn to Eliphalet, Elisha, Samuel, Joseph and Nathan Whiting sons to the decd. Bond: Mrs Elizabeth Whiting and Mr John Whiting "Bachr of Arts of ye Colo Scholl at New Haven"

[122] 21 Apr 1727 Letters of adm on est of Mr Hez Mason of Windham decd granted to Thomas Dimock. Bond: Mr Jonathan Bingham. Inv exh.

[122] 2 Jul 1729 Mr Thomas Dimmack adm of est of Mr Hez Mason of Windham decd exh acct.

[123] 13 Jun 1727 Will of Mr Joseph Woodward exh by exec Mr Richard Woodward (Mr John Woodward was also an exec but excused because of an accident he incurred)

[123] 29 Apr 1728 Mr Richard Woodward exec of Mr Joseph Woodward of Canterbury decd exh acct.

Windham (Conn.) Probate Records, Vol 1, Sect.2 (1719-1734)

[123] 21 Dec 1739 est of Mr Joseph Woodward of Windham decd.

[124] 26 Jun 1727 Letters of adm on est of Mr Caleb Conant of Windham decd granted to Mr Josiah Conant. Bond: Capt Thomas Storrs. Inv exh.

[124] 3 Mar 17__ Mr Josiah Conant adm of Mr Caleb Conant of Windham decd exh acct. 23 Jun 1734 ditto.

[125] 26 Jun 1727 Will of Mr Israel Luce of Windham decd exh by Mrs Grace Luce relict to decd and to Joseph Luce, execs. Inv exh. 9 May 1732 Mr Joseph Luce exec exh acct. 1 Mar 1733/4 ditto.

[126] 26 Jun 1727 Letters of adm on est of Mr Samuel Manning Jr of Windham decd granted to Mr Samuel Manning of sd Windham. Inv exh. 11 Jun 1728 adm exh acct.

[127] 27 Jun 1727 Will of Mr James Tisdall of Lebanon decd exh by execs. Inv exh. 28 Feb 1733/4 execs exh acct.

[128] 12 Sep 1727 Letters of adm on est of Isaac Parke of Plainfield decd granted to William Parke Jr of Plainfield. Inv exh. 8 Apr 1729 adm exh acct.

[129] 26 Sep 1727 Letters of adm on est of Mils Jurdon of Voluntown decd granted to Mrs Elezebeth Jurdon relict to sd decd. Inv exh. 6 May 1728 adm exh acct and Court grants support to widow.

[130] 9 Oct 1727 Letters of adm on est of Deacon Jacob Warrin of Plainfield decd granted to Mrs Sarah Warrin relict

Windham (Conn.) Probate Records, Vol 1,Sect.2 (1719-1734)

to sd decd and to Joseph Warrin of sd Plainfield. Inv exh. 13 Aug 1728 adm exh acct.

[131] 9 Oct 1727 Letters of adm on est of Mr John How of Plainfield decd granted to Mrs Phebe How relict to sd decd. Inv exh. 11 Jul 1732 Mrs Phebe How for bringing up youngest ch from 14 mos to 5 yrs old.

[132] 9 Oct 1727 Will of Mr Matthias Button of Plainfield decd exh. Inv exh.

[133] 10 Oct 1727 Letters of adm on est of Mr Jame Pinno of Lebanon decd granted to Mr John Newcomb and Mrs Dorothy Pinno of sd Lebanon. 12 Dec 1728 inv exh and acct exh.

[134] 10 Oct 1727 Letters of adm on est of Mr John Hutchason of Lebanon decd granted to Mr Samuel Hutchason and Mrs Helpsobeth Hutchason both of Lebanon. Inv exh. 23 Jun 1742 adms exh acct.

[135] 31 Oct 1727 Letters of adm on est of Mr Nathaniel Barkar of Windham decd granted to Mrs Elezebeth Barker relict to decd. 12 Sep 1732 inv exh.

[135] 12 Sep 1732 Mrs Elezebeth Badkuck widow and adm of est of Mr Nathaniel Barker decd. Exh acct. 5 Nov 1743 Mr Seth Cutler posted bond on est of Mr Nathaniel Barker of Windham decd. 5 Nov 1743 Amasa [Gleghuns?] gdn to Mary Barker posted bond and Quietus est granted.

[136] 4 Nov 1727 Letters of adm on est of Mr Samuel Lee of Killingly decd granted to Mrs Mary Lee and Mr John Lee. Inv exh. 12 Nov 1728 Mrs Mary Lee req more time. Jan 1728/9 Mrs Mary Lee exh acct.

Windham (Conn.) Probate Records, Vol 1, Sect.2 (1719-1734)

[137]   Letters of adm on est of Mr Jabez Allyn of Killingly decd granted to Mrs Mehetabell Allyn relict to decd. 22 Jan 1728/9 adm exh inv and acct.

[137]   20 Feb 1729/30 Mr John Hallwell and Mrs Mehetabell Halwell adm to est of Mr Jabez Alin of Killingly decd exh acct.

[138]   10 Nov 1727   Letters of adm on est of Mr Samuel Cleveland Jr of Canterbury decd granted to Mr John Bacon and Mrs Sarah Cleveland relict to decd. Inv exh. 9 Nov 1731 adms exh acct. 14 Jun 1743 adms exh acct.

[139]   20 Nov 1727   Letters of adm on est of Mr Simon Davis of Killingly decd granted to Mrs Sarah Davis relict to decd. Inv exh. 10 Jun 1729   Mrs Sarah Davis adm of Mr Simon Davis exh acct. 23 Oct 1730 Mrs Sarah Cooper late widow of Samll Davis of Killingly exh acct.

[140]   14 Nov 1727 Letters of adm on est of Mr Robert Millar of Voluntown decd granted to Mrs James Millar widow and Peter Millar of sd Voluntown.

[140]   25 Nov 1735   Mr Timothy Cooper (etc) adm of est of Mr Samuel Davis of Killingly exh acct. 14 Jun 1737 Quietus est granted on est.

[141]   14 Nov 1727   Will of Mr Tixwell Ensworth of Canterbury decd exh by Mr Joseph Ensworth and Mr Nathaniel Ensworth execs. 9 Jan 1728/29 Quietus est granted to Mr Thomas [sic] Ensworth and Mr Joseph Cleveland [sic] on est of Mr Tixwell Ensworth of Canterbury decd.

[142] 14 Nov 1727 Letters of adm on est of Mrs Mary How of Plainfield decd to Mr John Stevens of sd Plainfield. Inv

Windham (Conn.) Probate Records, Vol 1, Sect.2 (1719-1734)

exh. 3 Apr 1728 Mr John Stevens since decd. Court appts Mr John Parkhurst of Plainfield as adm.

[143] 14 Nov 1727 Letters of adm on est of Mr Ebenezer Whitny of Pomfret decd granted to Mrs Anna Whitney. 11 Jun 1728 Mrs Anna Whitney adm exh acct.

[144] 14 Nov 1727 Letters of adm on est of Mr John Carter of Canterbury decd granted to Mrs Mary Carter relict to sd decd. Inv exh. 6 Mary 1730 Mr [sic] Mary Bundy relict to Mr John Carter of Canterbury decd exh acct and quietus est granted.

[145] 19 Nov 1727 Letters of adm on est of Mr John Pike of Canterbury decd granted to Mrs Sarah Pike and Mr John Pike. 14 Jul 1730 Mr John Pike adm exh inv and acct.

[146] 14 Nov 1727 Letters of adm on est of Mr Josiah Spaulding of Plainfield decd granted to Mrs Sarah Spaulding relict to decd. 11 Nov 1729 adm exh inv and acct. 13 Jan 1729 adm exh acct.

[147] 14 Nov 1727 Letters of adm on est of Mr David Carver of Canterbury decd granted to Mr Solomon Pain of sd Canterbury. 3 Jan 1728/9 adm exh inv. 13 Feb 1728/9 adm exh acct and took out order for distribution of estate.

[148] 4 Dec 1727 Mr Samuel Harris adm of Mrs Elizabeth Harris of New London decd; land in Mansfield; inv. £70. Distributed to heirs of Mr Peter Harris of New London decd late husband of Elizabeth Harris decd. Mr Samuel Harris eld son; Mr Thomas Harris 2nd son; Mr Peter Harris 3rd son; Mr Stephen Harris 4th son; Mr Joseph Harris 5th son; Mrs Elizabeth _____ eld dau; Mrs Marcy _____ 2nd dau; Mrs Hannah _____ 3rd dau; Mrs Mary _____ 4th

Windham (Conn.) Probate Records, Vol 1,Sect.2 (1719-1734)

dau; Mrs Martha _____ 5th dau. Court appts Mr Thomas Storrs, Mr John Arnold; Mr Josiah Conant to distribute.

[149] 4 Dec 1727 Will of Mr Samuel Adams of Canterbury decd exh by Capt Joseph Adams of sd Canterbury exec.

[150] 12 Dec 1727 Letters of adm on the estate of the Rev. Mr Samuel Estarbrooks of Canterbury decd granted to Rev Mr John Fisk of Killingly and Rev. Mr Eleazur Williams of Mansfield. 9 Apr 1728 inv exh. 24 Apr 1729 acct exh; 15 Jul 1729 Quietus est granted.

[151] 15 Dec 1727 Letters of adm on the estate of Mr Jonathan Simons of Windham decd granted to Mrs Miriam Simons and Mr Jacob Simons Jr. Inv exh. 28 Feb 1733/4 acct exh.

[152] 18 Dec 1727 Letters of admin on the est of Mr Samuel Storrs of Mansfield decd granted to Mrs Martha Storrs relict to sd decd and Mr Samll Storrs and Mr John Storrs all of Mansfield. Inv exh.

[152] 18 Dec 1727 Rev Mr Eliezer Williams appt gdn to Joseph Storrs 4th son of decd, he desiring the same. Bond: Mr William Paine.

[153] 22 Nov 1727 Mr Thomas Ensworth and Mr Joseph Cleveland adm of Mr Tixwell Ensworth of Canterbury decd present inv £291.3.3 to be distr. Sons Mr John Ensworth decd; Joseph Ensworth; Ezra Ensworth; and, Nehemiah Ensworth have already received their share. Mrs Sarah Ensworth, relict to decd; son Mr Thomas Ensworth; Mrs Sarah Cleveland eld; Mrs Elizabeth White 2nd. Court appts Mr Samll Butt, Mr Solomon Tracy, Mr John Felch distributors. 9

Windham (Conn.) Probate Records, Vol 1,Sect.2 (1719-1734)

Jan 1727/8 Mr Thomas Ensworth, Mr Joseph Cleveland, Mrs Elizabeth White, widow present bond.

[154] 28 Dec 1727 Letters of adm on est of Mr Richard Gail of Canterbury decd granted to Mrs Sara Gail. Inv exh. 12 May 1730 Mrs Sarah Gail adm of Mr Richard Gail of Canterbury decd exh acct.

[155] 9 Jan 1727/8 Mr George Partridge adm of est of Mr Josiah Backar of Lebanon decd. Est £94.3.2. Distributed to: Samuel Backar, brother of decd; Joshua Backar brother of decd; Sarah Backar sister of decd; Elisha Backar brother of decd; Nathaniel Backar brother of decd. Court appts Ens Ephraim Kingsbury of Plainfield, Mrs Josiah Bartlett of Lebanon to distribute. Mr George Partridge appt gdn to Joshua Backar, Sarah Backar, Elisha Backar; Nathaniel Backar brothers and sister to sd Josiah Backar decd. 11 Jan 1727/8 Mr George Partridge posts bond.

[156] 9 Jan 1727/8 Letters of adm on the est of Mr John Lasell of Windham decd granted to Mr Joshua Lasell. Inv exh.

[157] 13 Feb 1727/8 Mr Solomon Pain adm of est of Ens David Carver of Canterbury decd exh acct £2036.15.10 to be distributed. Court distr: Mrs Sarah Carver relict to decd; Mr Samuel Carver eld son; Jonathan Carver 2nd son; David Carver 3rd son; Benjamin Carver 4th son; Sarah Pain eld dau; Hannah Carver 2nd dau. Court appts Capt Joseph Adams, Mr Solomon Tracy, Mr John Felch all of Canterbury distributors. Court appts Mr John Dyer of Canterbury gdn to Jonathan Carver, David Carver, and Hannah Carver they desiring the same. Court appts Mr Solomon Pain of Canterbury gdn to Benjamin Carver. Mr John Dyer posts bond.

Windham (Conn.) Probate Records, Vol 1,Sect.2 (1719-1734)

[158] [no date] Mr Solomon Pain posts bond

[159] 13 Feb 1727/8 Letters of adm on est of Mr John Brown of Canterbury decd granted to Mrs Abigail Brown relict to sd decd. Inv. exh.

[160] 13 Mar 1728 Mrs Bashua Lovejoy adm to the est of Mr John Lovejoy of Plainfield decd. Amount to be distr: £34.8.1 movable and £390 real estate. Court distributes to: Mrs Bashua Lovejoy relict to decd; Benjamin Lovejoy eld son; Richard Lovejoy 2nd son; Elizabeth Lovejoy eld dau; Ann Lovejoy 2nd dau; Naomi Lovejoy 3rd dau; Freelove Lovejoy 4th dau. Court appts Ens Ephraim Kingsbury, Deacon Samuel Sterns, Mr Jonathan Parkhurst of Plainfield distributors. Court appts Mr Samuel Spaulding of Plainfield gdn to Richard Lovejoy; Mr John Parkhurst of Plainfield gdn to Ann Lovejoy she desiring same; Mr Ephraim Spaulding of Plainfield gdn to Naomi Lovejoy; and Mrs Bashua Lovejoy widow of Plainfield gdn to Freelove Lovejoy.

[161] all above guardians post bond

[162] 10 Apr 1728 Mrs Joan Millar and Pettar Millar adm of the est of Mr Robert Millar of Voluntown decd exh acct. To be distributed: £206.8.3. Court distr to: Mrs Joan Millar; Peter Millar eld son; Daniel Millar 2nd son; Eliek Sander Milar 3rd son; Margaret Hannah eld dau; James Millar son 4th son; Joan Millar 2nd dau. Court appts Deac. Jacob Bacon of Voluntown, Mr William Dean, and Mr William Marsh of Plainfield distributors.

[163] blank page

[164] 12 Mar 1728 Mr John Stevens adm on the est of Mary How of Plainfield, exh acct: £56.06.10 to be distr to: Mr

Windham (Conn.) Probate Records, Vol 1, Sect.2 (1719-1734)

Samuel How eld son; heirs of John How decd 2nd son; Mrs Sarah Whelar dau; Mrs Mary Russill; heirs of Mrs Hanah Cory decd dau; Mrs Deborah Munroo dau; Mrs Abigail Parkhurst dau; Mrs Elizabeth Stevens dau. Court appts Deac Samll Sterns, Ens Ephraim Kingsbury and William Marsh all of Plainfield to distribute. Court appts Mrs Phoebe How relict of John How decd gdn to the children; and Mr John Parkhurst of Plainfield appt gdn to Isaac Cory Jr son to sd Hannah Cory decd. 10 Apr 1728 Court appts Mr Isaac Cory of Plainfield gdn to his two sons Josia and Joseph Cory they desiring the same, they are sons of Hannah Cory decd.

[165] 12 Mar 1728 Mrs Phoebe How, widow, bond.

[165] 12 Mar 1728 Mr Isaac Cory bond.

[166] 20 Apr 1728 Mr John Storrs of Mansfield adm of est of Mr Samll Storrs of Mansfield decd exh acct: £1703.7.0 to be distributed. Martha, eldest dau already received her share. Mrs Martha Storrs relict to decd; Mrs Samuel Storrs eld son; Mr John Storrs 2nd son; Mr Hugens Storrs 3rd son; Mr Joseph Storrs 4th son; Mrs Martha Badcock eld dau; Mrs Elizabeth Storrs 2nd dau; Mrs Mary Storrs 3rd dau. Court appts Capt Thomas Storrs, Mr John Arnold, Mr Josiah Conant distributors.

[167] 29 Apr 1728 Letters of admin on est of Mr Stephen Frost of Canterbury decd granted to Mr Stephen Frost. Inv. exh.; 12 Mar 1730 acct exh.

[168] 2 May 1728 will of Mr John Sprague of Lebanon decd exh by his widow Mrs Lois Sprague exec. 16 Dec 1731 Mr Ralph Wheelock attorney for Lois Sprague exh acct.

Windham (Conn.) Probate Records, Vol 1, Sect.2 (1719-1734)

[168] 28 Jul 1729 Capt Ephraim Sprague exec of Mr Samuel Sprague of Lebaon decd exh acct.

[169] 6 May 1728 Will of Mr Joshua Stevens of Plainfield decd exh by execs Mr Ephraim Kingsbury and Mrs Elizabeth Stevens relict to sd decd; 19 Jan 1728/9 inv exh; 8 Jan 1733/4 acct exh.

[169] 6 Apr 1728 Letters of admin on est of Mrs Hannah Ballard of Plainfield decd granted to Rev Mr Eliezur Williams of Mansfield.

[170] 3 Jun 1728 Letters of admin on the est of Mrs Rebeckah Estarbrooks relct to Rev Mr Samuel Estarbrooks of Canterbury decd granted to Rev Mr Eliezur Williams of Mansfield. 15 Jul 1729 Rev Mr Eleazur Williams states no estate found and Quietus est granted.

[171] 12 Jun 1728 Mr James Welch adm of Mr James Welch of Plainfield decd exh acct: £78.4.4 to be distributed. Mary Welch widow; Ebenzer Welch and John Welch already received from their father; Mr James Welch eld son; Samll Welch 2nd son; Thomas Welch 3rd son; Elizabeth Lawrence eld dau; Mary Spaulding 2nd dau; Martha Welch 3rd dau. Court appts Mr John Felows, Mr Ebenezer Harris, and Mr Philip Bump all of Plainfield distributors.

[172] 11 Jun 1728 Letters of adm on est of Bartholomew Williams of Plainfield decd granted to Catherine Williams of Plainfield. 11 Nov 1729 Catherine Williams exh inv. 11 Nov 1729 Quietus Est granted.

[173] 27 Jun 1728 Letters of adm on the est of Mr Robert Badcock of Windham decd granted to Caleb Badcock of Windham and to Mr Thomas Porter of Coventry (sons of the

Windham (Conn.) Probate Records, Vol 1, Sect.2 (1719-1734)

decd). Inv. exh. 28 Jun 1732 Mr Thomas Porter of Mansfield adm of Mr Robert Badcock decd exh acct and granted Quietus Est.

[174] 27 Jun 1728 Will of Mr Steven Tilden of Lebanon decd exh by son Stephen Tilden. Inv exh. 3 Jul 1729 Mr Stephen Tilden adm of Steven Tilden exh acct.

[174] Will of Mr John Read of Windham exh by execs. Inv. exh.

[175] 26 Jul 1728 Last will of Mr Stephen Tilden of Lebanon decd distr to children: Stephen Tilden, Mary Powel, and Hannah Tilden; Mr Roland Powell and Mr Caleb Pierce husbands of sd Mary and Hannah daughters of the decd. Court appts Mr Richard Abbe of Windham, Mr Josiah Conant of Mansfield, and Mr Stephen Strong of Lebanon to divide est.

[176] 6 Aug 1728 Will of Hosea Joyce of Mansfield exh by exec. 16 Sep 1728 Inv exh.

[176] 11 Nov 1728 Letters of admin on the est of Mr William Brustar of Lebanon decd granted to Mrs Patience Brustar relict to decd.

[177] 29 Nov 1728 Mrs Anna Whitney adm of Mr Ebenezer Whitney of Pomfret decd exh acct, to be distributed: £647.18.8. To Mrs Anna Whitney relict; Ezekel Whitney eld son; Zachariah Whitney 2nd son; Enoch Whitney 3rd son; Israel Whitney 4th son; Ebenezer Whitney 5th son; Anna Whitney dau. Court appts Capt Grosvenor of Pomfret, Capt Joseph Adams and Mr Deliverance Brown of Canterbury distributors.

Windham (Conn.) Probate Records, Vol 1,Sect.2 (1719-1734)

[178] 10 Dec 1728 Mr Stephen Strong of Lebanon appt gdn to David Royce a minor son of Jonathan Royce of Lebanon decd.

[178-9] 12 Dec 1728 Mr Samll Maning adm of est of Mr Samuel Maning Jr of Windham decd exh acct, to be distr: £118.13.0 to Josiah Maning eld son; Hez Maning 2nd son; Samuel Maning 3rd son; David Maning 4th son; Abigail Maning eld dau; Sarah Maning 2nd dau. Court appts Capt Eleazer Cary, Mr Samll Palmour, Mr John Spencer distr. Hez Ripley appt gd to Hez, Abigail, Sarah, Samuel Maning minors; Mr Samuel Maning appt gdn to Josiah Maning minor; Mr Samll Cook appt gdn to David Maning minor.

[180] 9 Dec 1728 Letters of adm on the est of Mr Jacob Spaulding of Killingly decd granted to Mrs Hanah Spaulding relict. 4 Dec 1729 inv exh. 9 Jun 1730 Mrs Hanah Spaulding exh acct. 11 Mar 1735 Mr Edwrd Stewart adm to est of Jacob Spaulding of Killingly decd exh acct. 22 Nov 1735 same as 11 Mar. 29 Dec 1735 a Quietus Est granted.

[181] 14 Jan 1728/9 Mrs Martha Storrs relict of Mr Samll Storrs of Mansfield decd is herself decd. Her inheritance to be distr to: Samuel Storrs eld son; John Storrs 2nd son; Hugins Storrs 3rd son; Joseph Storrs 4th son; heirs of Martha Badcock decd eld dau; Mary Jacobs 3rd dau; Elizabeth Storrs 2nd dau. Court appts: Capt Thomas Storrs, Mr Josiah Conant, John Arnold distributors.

[182] 13 Jan 1728/9 Letters of adm on the est of Mrs Hanah Rigbe widow of Plainfield decd granted to Mr Joseph Parkhurst. 13 Jan 1728/9 Mr Joseph Parkhurst of Plainfield appt gdn to Susanna Rigbe minor dau of Mr Jonathan Rigbe of Plainfield decd. 14 Aug 1729 Mr Joseph Parkhurst adm of Mrs Hanah Rigbe exh acct.

Windham (Conn.) Probate Records, Vol 1,Sect.2 (1719-1734)

[183] 22 Jan 1728/9 Letters of adm on the est of Mr Ebenezer Green of Killingly decd granted to Mr Henry Green of Killingly. Inv. exh.

[183] 11 Feb 1728/9 Will of Mr James Danielson of Killingly exh by Mr Samll Danielson. Inv exh.

[184] 11 Feb 1728/9 Will of Mr Samll Adams of Canterbury decd. He had 7 children, 1 grandchild [unnamed]. Adm is Capt Joseph Adams.

[185] 11 Feb 1728/9 Letters of adm on est of Ann Lovejoy of Plainfield decd granted to Samuel Spaulding. 18 Feb 1728/9 inv exh. 9 Sep 1729 acct exh. 11 May 1742 acct exh.

[186] 24 Apr 1729 Letters of adm on the est of Mr John Haskall of Killingly decd granted to Mr John King of Tanton [i.e. Taunton, Mass.] with Mr John Haskall eld son of decd desiring the same. 20 Feb 1730/1 inv exh. 20 Feb 1730/1 Capt John King adm exh acct.

[187] 7 Jul 1729 Letters of adm on the est of Mr Gershom Hall of Mansfield decd granted to Mr Isaac Hall of Mansfield. Inv exh. 9 Jun 1730 Isaac Hall exh acct. 14 Jul 1730 Isaac Hall exh acct.

[188] 2 Jul 1729 Will of Mr James Kidder of Mansfield decd exh by Mr James Kidder exec.

[188] 2 Jul 1729 Will of William More of Windham decd exh by exec [unnamed]

[189] 3 Jul 1729 Will of Mr Benjamin Woodworth of Lebanon decd exh by Mr Benjamin Woodworth exec.

Windham (Conn.) Probate Records, Vol 1, Sect.2 (1719-1734)

[189] 8 Jul 1729 Will of Mr William Rogers of Voluntown decd exec [unnamed] 4 Dec 1729 inv exh.

[190] 8 Jul 1729 Will of Mr Richard Dresser of Killingly decd exh by exec Mrs Marcy Dresser relict and Jacob Dresser. Inv exh.

[191] 15 Jul 1729 Rev Mr John Fisk and Rev Mr Eleazer Williams adm of est of Rev Mr Samll Estarbrooks of Canterbury decd; the exec of the will was Mrs Rebeckah Estarbrooks relict of decd also decd. Court appts Rev Mr Eleazer Williams of Mansfield exec. Est is intestate. 14 Jul 1730 Rev Mr Eleazer Williams exh acct.

[192] 24 Aug 1729 Will of Rev Mr Peter Thatcher of Milton [Mass] is exh.

[193] 24 Aug 1729 Will of Mrs Susannah Thatcher decd relict of Rev Mr Peter Thatcher of Milton is exh.

[194] 16 Jan 1729/30 Letters of adm of Mr Archable Mackdoaool late of Ireland and belonging to Voluntown granted to Mr William Mackdowell of Voluntown brother of the decd. 12 Jan 1730/1 inv exh. 12 Jan 1730/1 delay granted.

[195] 3 Feb 1729/30 Will of Mr Benjamin Duffty exh by exec Mrs Elizabeth Douffty and Mr Barnabus Case and Mr Jacob Lilly. 26 Feb 1729/30 Mr Jacob Lilly exh acct.

[195] 3 Feb 1729/30 Letter of adm on the est of Mr Benjamin Douffty of Windham decd granted to Mr Barnard Case, Mr Jacob Lillie, and Mrs Elizabeth Doufty widow. 13 Nov 1735 Mr Jacob Lillie exh acct.

Windham (Conn.) Probate Records, Vol 1, Sect.2 (1719-1734)

[196] 20 Feb 1729/30 Mr John Halwell and Mrs Mehetabel Hallwell appt gdn to Elizabeth Alin, Mary Alin, Mehetabel Alin minor daus to Jabez Alin of Killingly decd. John and Mehitabel Alin [sic] give bond.

[196] 3 Mar 1730 Will of Mr Joseph Eton of Killingworth exh by Mrs Hana Eton widow. 26 Feb 1730/1 Mrs Hannah Eaton exec appeared by her atty Mr Jonathan Crane exh acct. 29 Jun 1733 exh acct. 26 Jun 1741 exh acct.

[197] 3 Mar 1730 Will of Mr Elisha Dunham of Mansfield decd granted to John Arnold and Mrs Temperance Dunham widow both of sd Mansfield. Inv exh. 27 Feb 1739/40 Mrs Temperance Dunham adm, exh acct.

[197] 24 Feb 1741/2 Mr Benjamin Daufty est acct exh.

[198] 17 Mar 1730 Letters of adm on the est of Mr Thomas Bingham of Windham decd granted to Mr Jonathan Bingham of Windham. Inv exh. 27 Jun 1734 a Quietus Est granted on est of Thomas Bingham.

[199] 10 Mar 1730 Will of Mr Thomas Grosvenor exh by exec.

[200] 9 Jun 1730 Edward Whelar minor son of Mr Ephraim Whelar of Plainfield decd chose Mr Matthew Huntington of Norwich as his gdn.

[201] 14 Jul 1730 Letters of adm on the est of David Dill of Voluntown granted to Mrs Mary Dill widow and relict to decd. Inv exh. 8 Aug 1738 widow exh acct including costs of bring up younger children to age of five.

Windham (Conn.) Probate Records, Vol 1, Sect.2 (1719-1734)

[202] 26 Aug 1730 Letters of adm on the est of Mrs Hannah Woodward of Canterbury decd relict and widow of Mr Joseph Woodward of Canterbury decd granted to Mr Nathaniel Richards of Norwich. 31 Dec 1731 inv exh. 26 Aug 1730 Nathaniel Richards appt gdn to Joseph Woodward minor son of Mr Joseph Woodward decd.

[203] 1 Sep 1730 Letters of adm on the est of Mr Ebenezer Hebard of Windham decd granted to Mr Robert Hebard and Mr Joseph Hebard. 1 Dec 1730 inv exh. 9 Jan 1732/3 acct exh. 23 Feb 1736/7 acct exh. 29 Jun 1737 a Quietus Est granted.

[204] 23 Sep 1730 Will of Mr Robert Mason of Ashford decd exh by Hanah Mason relict to sd decd. 8 Dec 1730 inv exh. 8 Nov 1737 acct exh by exec.

[204] 29 Sep 1730 Will of Mr Nathaniel Juell of Plainfield decd exh by execs Mr David Whitney and Mrs Sarah Juell. 13 Mar 1732 acct exh.

[205] 3 Oct 1730 Will of Mrs Mary Saltonstall of Boston [Mass.] decd exh by one of the execs Mr William Clark.

[205] 5 Oct 1730 Will of Mr Jonah Palmour of Windham decd exh by Mr John Spencer exec. 23 Feb 1731/2 acct exh.

[206] 10 Nov 1730 Will of Mr Ebenezer Grosvenor of Pomfret decd exh by execs. Inv. exh.

[206] 25 Nov 1730 Letters of adm on est of Mr Nathan Right of Ashford decd granted to Mrs Dorothy Right relict of sd decd. 14 Sep 1731 acct exh.

Windham (Conn.) Probate Records, Vol 1, Sect.2 (1719-1734)

[207] 8 Dec 1730 Letters of adm on est of Mr Benjamin Scott of Windham decd granted to Mary Scott relict of the decd. Inv exh.

[207] 8 Jul 1735 Execs of est of Mr Nathaniel Juell of Plainfield decd exh acct.

[208] 10 Dec 1730 Mary Estarbrook minor dau of Rev Mr Samuel Estarbrooks chose Mrs Sarah Hubbard of Mansfield as gdn.

[209] 10 Dec 1730 Nathan Hebard minor son of Ebenezer Hebard of Windham decd chose Mr Joseph Hebard gdn.

[210] 21 Dec 1730 On 10 Nov 1726, one third of the est of Mr Samll Shepard was distr to Mrs Eleanor Shepard relict of sd decd and she is now decd. Her share is distr: Jonathan Shepard eld son; David Shephard 2nd son; Nathan Shepard 3rd son; Benjamin Shephard 4th son; Eleanor Derby eld dau; Mary Jonson 2nd dau; Luce 3rd dau. Ct appts Joseph Lawrence, Thomas Gallup, John Crery as distr.

[211] 20 Jan 1730/1 Will of Mr John Broughton of Windham decd exh by his execs. Inv exh. 14 Jan 1734/5 exec of Mr John Broughton exh acct.

[211] 26 Feb 1730/1 Letters of adm on est of Mrs Grace Luce of Windham decd granted to Mr Joseph Luce. Inv exh. 9 May 1732 Joseph Luce exh acct.

[212] 9 Mar 1731 John Chapman minor son of John Chapman of Ashford decd chose Capt John Perry as gdn.

[213] 8 May 1731 Samll How minor son of John How decd chose Mr John Parkhurst as gdn.

Windham (Conn.) Probate Records, Vol 1,Sect.2 (1719-1734)

[213] 12 May 1731 Letters of adm on est of Mr Benjamin Phelps of Mansfield decd granted to Mr Joseph Phelps and Mr Jedediah Phelps (widow refused adm) Inv exh. 28 Jun 1732 execs exh acct.

[214] 8 June 1731 Will of Mr Robert Buswill of Canterbury exh by Mr John Felch adm. 12 Sep 1733/4 acct exh.

[214] 5 Dec 1731 Letters of adm on the est of Jonathan Palmour of Windham decd granted to Mrs Sarah Palmour relict of the decd. Inv exh. 25 Jun 1735 acct exh.

[215] 11 Jan 1731/2 Letters of adm on the est of Mr Joseph Grifon of Pomfret decd granted to Mr Benjamin Griffen and Mrs Margaret Griffen of sd Pomfret. Inv exh. 14 Feb 1737/8 acct exh; 12 Jan 1741/2 family use granted; 13 Apr 1742 Quietus est granted.

[216] 8 Feb 1731/2 Will of Mr Edward Walker of Ashford decd exh by two of execs: Mrs Mary Walker and Deac. Kendall. Inv exh. 15 Dec 1732 Deac. Isaac Kendall exh acct.

[217] 23 Feb 1731/2 Will of Mr Thomas Rugg of Mansfield decd exh by exec Mrs Elizabeth Rugg who refuses adm. Court appts Mr Stephen Brown of Windham adm. Inv exh. 13 Mar 1733 acct exh.

[218] 29 Feb 1731/2 Letters of adm on est of Mr Zebediah Abbott of Windham decd granted to Mr Philllip Abbott of sd Windham; 13 Mar 1732 inv exh; 13 May 1733 acct exh; 12 Feb 1733/4 Quietus est granted.

[219] 13 Mar 1732 Will of Mr William Durke of Windham decd exh by execs Mrs Rebeckah Durk and William Durk.

Windham (Conn.) Probate Records, Vol 1, Sect. 2 (1719-1734)

Inv exh. 13 Mar 1733 allowed to widow for raising the yougest children to five.

[219] 4 Apr 1732 Letters of adm on the est of Mr John Stedman of Lebanon decd granted to Mr Josiah Dewey and Mrs Experience Stedman widow. Inv exh.

[220] 29 Jun 1732 Letters of adm on the est of Mr William Ticknor of Lebanon decd granted to Mr William Ticknor son of the decd. Inv exh.

[220] 8 Apr 1735 Mr Josiah Dewey adm of est of Mr John Stedman decd exh acct.; 27 Jun 1733 same; 28 Feb 1733/4 same including wid charges for bringing up the youngest child two years.

[221] 1 Jun 1732 Mr Stephen Brown of Windham exec of est of Mr Thomas Rug of Mansfield decd, estate is insolvent. Court appts Capt Thomas Storrs, Mr Josiah Conant, and Mr Joseph Jacobs to deal with creditors.

[221] 9 Jul 1735 Mr Josiah Dewey Jr adm on est of Mr John Stedman of Lebanon granted a quietus est.

[222] 30 Jun 1732 Will of Andrew Warner of Mansfield decd exh by exec.

[222] 227 Jul 1732 Letters of adm on est of Mr Nathaniel Ayrs of Voluntown decd granted to Mrs Presilah Ayrs relict. Inv exh. 9 Apr 1734 acct exh; 23 Apr 1734 acct exh.

[223] 12 Sep 1732 Will of Mr John Badcock of Windham decd exh by execs (one exec Mr Thomas Porter refused trust. Inv exh. 29 Jun 1733 Mrs Elizabeth Badcock exec exh acct.

Windham (Conn.) Probate Records, Vol 1,Sect.2 (1719-1734)

[224] 9 Jan 1732/3 Letters of adm on est of Mr James Hide Jr of Canterbury decd granted to Mrs Mary Hide relict of decd. 14 Jan 1734/5 act exh. 9 May 1738 acct exh.

[225] 1 Mar 1732/3 Mrs Phebe How adm of est of Mr John How acct £898 to distr to: Mrs Phebe How; Josiah How eld son; John How 2nd son; Samll How 3rd son; James How 4th son; Jonas 5th son; Luce How dau. Court appts Ens Ephraim Kingsbury, Mr David Lawrence and Mr Edward Spaulding distr.

[226] 1 Mar 1732/3 Court appt Mr Samll Spaulding gdn to James How minor son of Mr John How of Plainfield decd, he [James] desiring the same.

[226] 1 Mar 1732/3 Court appts Mrs Phebe How gdn to John How minor son of Mr John How of Plainfield decd he desiring the same and also to Jonas How minor son of decd.

[227] 13 Feb 1732/3 Letters of adm on est of Mr David Canada of Windham decd to Mr Nathaniel Philips and Mrs Margreet Canada both of Windham. Inv exh "in ye 2nd book of records."

[228] 13 Mar 1733 Letters of adm on the est of Mr Henry Farnnum of Windham decd granted to Mrs Phebe Uarnnum [sic] relict.

[229] 13 Mar 1733 Letters of adm on the est of Mr Joseph Bugbee of Ashford decd granted to Mr John Bugbee son of the decd.

[229] 13 Mar 1733 Will of Mr Thomas Huntington of Mansfield decd exh by one of execs: Mr Thomas Huntington. Inv exh. 28 Feb 1733/4 acct exh. 25 Feb 1735/6 acct exh.

Windham (Conn.) Probate Records, Vol 1, Sect.2 (1719-1734)

[230] 13 Mar 1733 Will of Mr Jacob Parker of Ashford decd exh. Inv exh.

[230] 10-Jun 1733 acct exh; 27 Jun 1734 acct exh.

[231] 10 Apr 1733 Will of Mr Caleb Chappell of Lebanon decd exh by exec Caleb Chappell. Inv exh.

[231] 10 Apr 1733 Letters of adm on the est of Mr Samll Paine of Pomfret decd granted to Mr Samll Pain son to decd and to Mr Seth Pain of Pomfret. Inv. exh. 10 Sep 1734 acct exh.

[232] 1 May 1733 Letters of adm on the est of Mr Joseph Covell of Killingly decd granted to Mr Stephen Covell. Inv exh.

[232] 22 Jun 1733 Letters of adm on the est of Mr Richard Adams of Canterbury granted to Mr John Adams and Mrs Mary Adams of Canterbury. Inv exh. 9 Apr 1734 acct exh.

[233] 12 Jun 1733 Will of Mr Thomas Gallup of Plainfield decd exh by execs John Crery and Nathaniel Gallup. Inv exh. 3 Apr 1736 acct exh.

[233] 9 Jul 1733 Will of Mr Jonathan Jennings of Windham decd exh by execs Mr Richard Abbe Esq and Mr Ebenezer Jennings. Inv exh.

[234] 28 Jun 1733 Letters of adm on the est of Mr Daniel Denison of Windham decd granted to Mrs Hanah Denison relict of decd. Inv exh. 27 Jun 1734 acct exh.

Windham (Conn.) Probate Records, Vol 1, Sect.2 (1719-1734)

[234] 27 Jun 1733 Will of Mr Jedediah Strong of Lebanon decd exh by execs. Inv exh.

[235] 27 Jun 1733 Will of Rev Mr William Billings of Windham Village decd exh by execs. Inv exh. 4 Jun 1734 acct exh; 20 Jun 1743 acct exh.

[235] 8 Dec 1727 William Dean of Plainfield received of his brother John Dean of Groton as an exec of their father Mr James Dean of Plainfield decd.

[236] 14 Aug 1733 Court appts Mr Thomas Stevens 3rd gdn for John Stevens a minor son of Mr John Stevens decd of Plainfield.

[237] 1 Mar 1733/4 Will of Mr John Badcock of Windham decd. Exh acct incl £5 per year until five for youngest children.

[237] 1 Mar 1733/4 Mrs Elizabeth Badcock widow and relict of Mr John Badcock of Windham decd, granted support.

[238] 9 Apr 1734 Mr Deliverance Brown of Canterbury appt gdn to Luce Adams a minor dau of Mr Richard Adams of Canterbury decd. 9 Apr 1734 Quietus est granted.

[239] 23 Apr 1734 Widow of Mr Nathaniel Ayrs of Voluntown granted support. 24 Sep 1734 exh acct. 12 Jul 1737 exh acct.

[240] 11 Sep 1733 Will of Mr John Preston of Windham decd exh by executrix. Inv exh. 9 Jul 1734 acct exh. 8 Nov 1738 acct exh.

Windham (Conn.) Probate Records, Vol 1, Sect.2 (1719-1734)

[241] 4 Jun 1734 Mr James Otis of New London appt gdn to Patience Billings minor dau of Rev Mr William Billings of Windham Village decd.

[242] 28 Feb 1728/9 Mr Thomas Hunt of Lebanon Jr appt gdn to Samuel Wadsworth a minor son to Mr Samll Wordsworth [sic]

[243] 10 Sep 1734 Mr Philip Abbot of Windham appt gdn to Joseph Leach, a minor son of Mr James Leach of Windham decd, he desiring the same.

[243 2nd] 10 Sep 1734 Mr Joseph Larance of Plainfield appt gdn to Nathan Shephard, a minor son to Samuel Shepard of Plainfield, he desiring the same.

[243 2nd] 14 Jul 1741 Administratrix of Mr John Brown of Canterbury requested distr by Court. To Mrs Abigal White [sic] late widow to Mr John Brown; Jabez Brown eld son; Abigail Brown dau. Court appts Deac Benjamin Bigsbe, Capt William Chandler both of Killingly in Thomas [i.e. Thompson] Parish, distributors.

[244] 10 Sep 1734 Exec of Mr John Badcock of Windham decd assisted by Mr Nathaniel Sestions of Pomfret sells some land pursuant to an act of the General Assembly 9 May 1734.

Windham (Conn.) Probate Records, Vol 1 (1719-1734)

**all ministers in town 50
**brick south church 50
**Church of God in Ashford 60
**Harvard College 50
**ministers of "new old south church" 50
**poor of "new old south church" 50
**poor of town of Boston 50
*HAGAR 45
*HAGAR, MY NEGRO WOMAN 45
*HAGAR, NEGRO WOMAN 45
*INDIAN GIRL 39
*JENNY 45
*LITTLE SAMBOO, MY NEGRO SERVANT 45
*MY NEGROES 50
*NATAHANK, Margaret 45
*NEGRO MAN PETER 61
*NEGRO MAN SERVANT 55
*NEGRO MAN SERVANT 8
*PETER NEGRO MAN 62
*SAMBO 45
*SLAVES
"INDIAN CHILD" 23
"INDIAN MAN" 23
"INDIAN WOMAN" 23
"NEGRO MAN" 23
ABBE, Ebenezer 59
ABBE, John 53 61
ABBE, Joshua 59 62
ABBE, Mary 56
ABBE, Richard 6 14 17 18 28 36 41 51 52 53 55 56 58 61 62 81 82 88 98 108
ABBE, Thomas 47
ABBOTT, Nathaniel 6 7 55 60
ABBOTT, Phillip 105 110
ABBOTT, Zebediah 57 105
ABBOTT, Zebulon 56
ADAMS, Abigail 33
ADAMS, Chael? 11
ADAMS, Henry 33 82
ADAMS, Isaac 11
ADAMS, John 11 21 79 108
ADAMS, Joseph 7 8 15 17 21 32 33 34 40 42 49 83 93 94 98 100
ADAMS, Justice 42
ADAMS, Luce 109
ADAMS, Margaret 33
ADAMS, Mary 11 108
ADAMS, Michael 11 79
ADAMS, Richard 11 51 79 108 109
ADAMS, Ruth 11
ADAMS, Samuel 11 33 39 93 100
ADAMS, Thomas 33

Windham (Conn.) Probate Records, Vol 1 (1719-1734)

AINSWORTH see ENSWORTH
ALDEN, Andrew 23
ALLEN, Elizabeth 102
ALLEN, Jabez 39 91 102
ALLEN, Mary 102
ALLEN, Mehitabel 91 102
ALLEN, Samuel 58
ALLEN, William 75
APPLETON, Samll 50
ARDAWAY, Rebeca 85
ARDEWAY, Jacob 85
ARDUA, Daniel 69
ARDUA, Jacob 69
ARDUA, John 69
ARDUA, Mary 69
ARDUA, Rachel 69
ARDUA, Sarah 69
ARDWAY, Jacob 32
ARNOLD, John 32 38 93 96 99 102
AYERS, Nathaniel 58
AYRS, Nathaniel 87 106 109
AYRS, Presilah 106
BABBIDGE, Benja 51
BACKAR see BAKER
BACKER see BAKER
BACKUS, John 24 57 88
BACKUS, John 88
BACKUS, Sybil 24 25 88
BACKUS, Timothy 11
BACON, Jacob 30 95
BACON, John 54 91
BADCOCK, Benjamin 58
BADCOCK, Caleb 97
BADCOCK, Ebenezer 58
BADCOCK, Elizabeth 106
BADCOCK, Elizabeth 59 60 90 106 109
BADCOCK, John 38 59 65 106 109 110
BADCOCK, Jonathan 44
BADCOCK, Josiah 59 65
BADCOCK, Martha 38 41 59 65 96 99
BADCOCK, Mary 44
BADCOCK, Nathaniel 59
BADCOCK, Robert 36 58 97 98
BADCOCK, unborn 59
BAILEY, John 45
BAKER, Elisha 33 94
BAKER, Isaac 33
BAKER, Joshua 33 94
BAKER, Josiah 23 85 94
BAKER, Nathaniel 33 94
BAKER, Samuel 33 94
BAKER, Sarah 33 94
BALDWIN, John 38
BALLARD, Bethia 19
BALLARD, Enoch 7 54 76
BALLARD, Hannah 7 52 97
BALLARD, Hepsebah 7 54
BALLARD, Humphrey 76
BALLARD, Peleg 7 19 54 76
BALLARD, Thomas 7 54

Windham (Conn.) Probate Records, Vol 1 (1719-1734)

BALLARD, William 7 54 76
BARKER see also BAKER
BARKER, Dorothy 19
BARKER, Elizabeth 90
BARKER, Frances 80
BARKER, Francis 19 29
BARKER, Judith 19 29 30
BARKER, Martha 19 80
BARKER, Mary 90
BARKER, Nathaniel 14 60 90
BARNETT, John 6
BARROWS, Robert 63
BARTLETT, Josiah 33
BASS, John 29 70
BATEMAN, Ebenezer 61
BATEMAN, Eleazer 5 7 13 39 71 74
BATTLE, Katherine 50
BERRY, John 55
BETTIS, Thomas 21 84
BEWELL, Peter 7
BIGSBE, Benjamin 110
BILL, Jonathan 23
BILLINGS, Patience 110
BILLINGS, William 109 110
BINGHAM, Abel 57
BINGHAM, Gideon 58
BINGHAM, Jabez 57
BINGHAM, Jonathan 57 58 69 77 85 88 102
BINGHAM, Joseph 36 58 85

BINGHAM, Samuel 4 27 53 58 75
BINGHAM, Stephen 58
BINGHAM, Thomas 47 48 57 102
BIXBY, Benjamin 7 9 34 39 46
BLACKMAN, Elisha 10 72
BLACKMAN, Elizabeth 72 78
BLACKMAN, Joseph 2 72 78
BLISS, John 8 77
BLISS, Nathaniel 32
BLODGETT, Sarah 30
BLODGETT, William 3 10
BLOGGETT, Sarah 26 27
BLOGGETT, Willliam 26
BLOGGIT, Sarah 86
BLUNT, Ambrose 19 80
BOLEN, Jeremiah 28
BOND, Nathaniel 18
BOSWELL, Mary 54
BOSWELL, Mehitabel 54
BOSWELL, Moses 54
BOSWELL, Robert 54
BOSWELL, Thomas 54
BOWEN, Henry 21
BOWMAN, Francis 56
BRADFORD, Joseph 82
BRANDON, Joseph 50 51
BRANDON, Martha 50
BRANDON, Sarah 50

Windham (Conn.) Probate Records, Vol 1 (1719-1734)

BREWSTER, Benjamin 27 43
BREWSTER, Ebenezer 43
BREWSTER, Patience 43 98
BREWSTER, Peter 43
BREWSTER, Samuel 43
BREWSTER, William 43 98
BROOKS, Ebenezer 46
BROOKS, John 55
BROUGHTON, Abigail 52
BROUGHTON, John 104
BROUGHTON, John 52 53 76
BROUGHTON, Samuel 52
BROUGHTON, Tabitha 61
BROUGHTON, Thomas 52
BROWN, Abigail 21 95 110
BROWN, Chester? 52
BROWN, Deliverance 1 11 12 21 34 40 71 98 109
BROWN, Ebenezer 71 72
BROWN, Eliezer 1 11 12 26
BROWN, Jabez 110
BROWN, John 38 95 110
BROWN, Rebecca 1 45
BROWN, Stephen 63 65 105 106
BROWN, Thomas 1 11 12 21 49 72 83
BRUSTAR see BREWSTER
BRYANT, Simon 34
BUGBEE, John 107
BUGBEE, Joseph 60 107
BUGBEE, Joshua 49
BUGBEE, Josiah 52
BUMP, Josiah 19
BUMP, Phillip 7 12 19 23 35 79 81 97
BUMP, Samuel 19 79
BUMP, Samuel 79
BUNDY, Mary 92
BURNAP, Abraham 19
BURNAP, Isaac 12 19 82
BURNAP, Jacob 12
BURNAP, John 12 17 19 82
BUSHNELL, Joseph 74
BUSHNELL, Nathan 4 74
BUSWILL, Robert 105
BUTLER, Samuel 67
BUTT, Samuel 7 31 32 33
BUTT, Samuel 93
BUTTON, Daniel 30
BUTTON, Mary 17 30 37
BUTTON, Mathias 30 31 47 90
BUTTON, Peter 17 30 37 47
BUTTON, Zerviah 30
CADY, Daniel 83
CADY, Hannah 54
CANADA, David 107
CANADA, Margreet 107

Windham (Conn.) Probate Records, Vol 1 (1719-1734)

CARBOUR see SCARBROUGH
CARBROUGH see SCARBROUGH
CARPENTER, Mary 20
CARPENTER, Daniel 20
CARTER, John 31 92
CARTER, Mary 92
CARVER, Benjamin 41 42 94
CARVER, David 32 41 42 92 94
CARVER, Hannah 41 42 94
CARVER, Jonathan 41 42 94
CARVER, Samuel 41 42 94
CARVER, Sarah 94
CARY, Abigail 59 73 74 75
CARY, Eleazer 6 16 17 28 29 42 61 75 99
CARY, Hannah 63 67 75
CARY, Henry 75
CARY, Isaac Jr 6
CARY, Jabez 63 75
CARY, John 63 73
CARY, John 87
CARY, Joseph 4 59 63 66 73 74 75
CARY, Mercy 63 73 75
CARY, Seth 63 73 75
CARY, Zerviah 63 66 75
CASE, Barnabus 101
CASE, Benjamin 47
CASE, Bernard 33 47
CASWELL, Frances 39
CATHCART, Robert 23
CHANDLER, Col. 11
CHANDLER, John 52
CHANDLER, Joseph 63
CHANDLER, William 110
CHAPLIN, Tamzen 6
CHAPMAN, John 57 81 104
CHAPPEL, Abijah 61
CHAPPEL, Caleb 61
CHAPPEL, Deborah 61
CHAPPEL, Jonathan 61
CHAPPEL, Joshua 61
CHAPPEL, Mary 61
CHAPPEL, Noah 61
CHAPPEL, Ruth 61
CHAPPELL, Caleb 108
CHAPPELL, Caleb 66
CHAPPELL, Jabez 66
CHAPPELL, Joshua 66
CHAPPELL, Lt Caleb 62
CHEDOL, George 60
CHRISTOPHERS, Elizabeth 50
CHURCH, Daniel 66
CHURCH, Jonathan 66
CHURCH, Samuel 66
CLAP, Neh. 45
CLAPP, Lydey 45
CLAPP, Nathaniel 45
CLAPP, Thomas 24
CLARK, Aaron 61 62

Windham (Conn.) Probate Records, Vol 1 (1719-1734)

CLARK, Benjamin 85
CLARK, Benoni 18 21
CLARK, Elizabeth 50
CLARK, Gershom 18 37 43 76
CLARK, Hannah 74
CLARK, Jonathan 18 50
CLARK, Joseph 18
CLARK, Mary 10 18 50 79
CLARK, Richard 50
CLARK, Susannah 62
CLARK, Thomas 18 50
CLARK, Timothy 18 76
CLARK, William 1 18 50 51 79 103
CLEVELAND, Abigail 20
CLEVELAND, Elizabeth 17
CLEVELAND, Joseph 20 24 76 80 83 91 93 94
CLEVELAND, Josiah 17
CLEVELAND, Samuel 34 91
CLEVELAND, Sarah 33 54 91 93
CLOUGH, Jonathan 9 67
COBB, Gideon 56 60
COBB, Henry 51
COBURN, Edward 5
COBURN, Hannah 5
COGGWELL, Samuel 23
COIT, Joseph 7
COLEMAN, Rev. 50
CONANT, Benajah 68
CONANT, Caleb 28 68 89
CONANT, Deacon 64
CONANT, Josiah 106
CONANT, Josiah 32 37 41 43 49 68 89 93 96 98 99
CONANT, Malatiah 68
COOK, Samll 28 99
COOPER, Sarah 91
CORBIN, Thomas 59 60
CORY, Hannah 96
CORY, Isaac 8 31 96
COVELL, Joseph 61 108
COVELL, Stephen 61 108
COY, Samuel 38
CRANE, Isaac 47
CRANE, Jonathan 4 36 73 82 102
CRERY, John 2 7 8 12 14 19 30 31 33 37 39 43 51 54 58 61 62 77 82
CROCKER, Samuel Jr 23
CROSS, James 62
CROSS, Jonathan 37
CROSS, Wade 58 64
CROWFUT, Ebenezer 77
CROWFUT, Joanna 77
CROWFUT, Samuel 77
CUSHMAN, Eleazer 27
CUSHMAN, Lydia 27
CUSHMAN, Ruth 27
CUSHMAN, Thomas 27 87
CUSHMAN, William 27
CUSHMAN, Zibiah 27
CUTLER, Isaac 61
CUTLER, Seth 90

Windham (Conn.) Probate Records, Vol 1 (1719-1734)

CUTTING, David 13 67 80
CUTTING, Elizabeth 80
DAFFTY see DUFFY
DANA, Jacob 63
DANIELSON, James 39 40 100
DANIELSON, Mary 39
DANIELSON, Samll 39 40 100
DARBIE, James 65
DARBY, Eleanor 24 54 104
DARBY, James 24
DARBYSHR, Eleanor 84
DARBYSHR, James 84
DAUFTY see DUFFY
DAUGHTY see DUFFY
DAVICE see DAVIS
DAVIS, Daniel 15 18
DAVIS, Dinah 1 12
DAVIS, Ebenezer 11 12
DAVIS, Elizabeth 15 18
DAVIS, Ephraim 15 18
DAVIS, Ephraim 78
DAVIS, Hannah 15 18
DAVIS, Jonathan 78
DAVIS, Jonathan 8 15 18
DAVIS, Mary 15 18
DAVIS, Samuel 34 91
DAVIS, Sarah 34 50 91
DAVIS,, Ebenezer 72
DAVIS/DAVICE
DAVISON, Daniel 58
DAWSON, Martha 58
DEAN, Abigail 63

DEAN, Elijah 63
DEAN, Francis 13
DEAN, Hannh 13
DEAN, James 13 20 62 80 109
DEAN, John 2 14 71 72 80 109
DEAN, Jonathan 12 13 30 61
DEAN, Joseph 55 79
DEAN, Mary 13
DEAN, Nathaniel 13 30 31 54
DEAN, Sarah 13 62
DEAN, William 2 13 14 95 109
DEEN see DEAN
DENE see DEAN
DENISON, Daniel 108
DENISON, Hanah 108
DERBY see DARBY
DEWEY, Joseph 57
DEWEY, Josiah 65 106
DEWEY, Nathaniel 44
DEWOLFE see DWOLFE
DILL, David 31 48 102
DILL, Mary 102
DILLINO see DELANO
DIMMACK see DIMMOCK
DIMMOCK, Ebenezer 70
DIMMOCK, Israel 70
DIMMOCK, Thomas 58 88
DIMMOCK, Timothy 70

Windham (Conn.) Probate Records, Vol 1 (1719-1734)

DIXON, John 42
DIXON, Robert 61
DIXSON, John 54
DOGET, John 10
DOGET, Sarah 10
DONE, Joseph 58 67
DORRANCE, Samuel 42
DOUGLAS, John 12 62
DOUGLAS, Mary 2 72
DOUGLAS, Pege 62
DOUGLAS, William 2 71 72
DRESSER, Abigail 46
DRESSER, Asa 46
DRESSER, Benjamin 46
DRESSER, Jacob 46 101
DRESSER, John 46
DRESSER, Jonathan 48
DRESSER, Joseph 46
DRESSER, Keziah 46
DRESSER, Marcy 101
DRESSER, Martha 46
DRESSER, Mary 46
DRESSER, Richard 46 101
DUFFY, Benjamin 47 48 101 102
DUFFY, Desire 47
DUFFY, Elizabeth 47 191
DUFFY, Margaret 47
DUFFY, Martha 47
DUNHAM, Ebenezer 26 48 87
DUNHAM, Elisha 43 48 102
DUNHAM, John 87
DUNHAM, Temperance 102
DUNKLEE, Nathaniel 56
DUPE, Naomi 6
DURK see DURKEE
DURKEE, Elizabeth 8 9
DURKEE, Hannah 56 66
DURKEE, Henry 56 66
DURKEE, Huldah 56
DURKEE, Jeremiah 9 78
DURKEE, John 8 9
DURKEE, Lucy 56
DURKEE, Rebeckah 56 105
DURKEE, Sarah 56
DURKEE, Thomas 8 22 23 59 78 84
DURKEE, William 56 66 78 105
DWIGHT, John 46
DWOLFE, Matthew 43
DWOLFE, Patience 43
DYER, John 7 32 41 94
EASTMAN, dau 60
EASTMAN, Philip 6 7 54 60
EATON, Catherine 47
EATON, Desire 47
EATON, Elizabeth 60
EATON, Hannah 47 102
EATON, Jonathan 46
EATON, Joseph 47 102
EATON, Marchont 47
EATON, Mary 47
EATON, Sarah 47

Windham (Conn.) Probate Records, Vol 1 (1719-1734)

EDGECOMBE, Thomas 34 35
EELLS, Joshua 85
ELLISON, Anna 45
ELLISON, Comfort 45
ELLISON, Elizabeth 45
ENGLISH, Richard 21
ENSWORTH, Elizabeth 76
ENSWORTH, Ezra 93
ENSWORTH, John 7 76 93
ENSWORTH, Joseph 76 91 93
ENSWORTH, Nathaniel 91 93
ENSWORTH, Sarah 33 93
ENSWORTH, Thomas 33 91 93 94
ENSWORTH, Tixwell 31 33 91 93
ESTABROOK, Hobart 42
ESTABROOK, Mary 42 104
ESTABROOK, Nehemian 42
ESTABROOK, Rebecca 42 97 101
ESTABROOK, Samll 34 42 70 93 97 101
ETON see EATON
FANNING, Thomas 87
FARAR, Mary 22
FARNUM, Henry 60 107
FARNUM, Phebe 107
FARWELL, Elizabeth 20
FARWELL, Isaac 20
FASSET, Benjamin 31 34 38 40 49 83
FASSIT, Joseph 64
FELCH, John 8 15 17 31 32 33 34 39 42 54 93 94 105
FELLOWS, Ephraim 19 51
FELLOWS, Isaac 51
FELLOWS, John 2 7 12 13 35 79 97
FENTON, Ebenezer 43
FISK, Ebenezer 56
FISKE, John 34 93 101
FISKE, Mr. 42
FITCH, Ann 24 25 88
FITCH, Bridgett 1 11 72
FITCH, Ebenezer 11 72
FITCH, Jabez 57
FITCH, John 10 18 23 25 26 41 44 51 88
FITCH, Joseph 24 82 88
FITCH, Nathaniel 28
FITCH, Peletiah 57
FITCH, Th___ 33
FLINT, Christian 36
FLINT, John 75
FLINT, Joshua 41 44
FOLLETT, Benjamin 20 55 70 86
FOWLE, John 5
FOWLER, Joseph 23 37 85
FRANKLIN, Benjamin 21 84
FRENCH, Abijah 62

121

Windham (Conn.) Probate Records, Vol 1 (1719-1734)

FRINK, Elias 34
FROST, Huldah 69
FROST, Stephen 8 35 69 83 96
FULLER, Constant 36
FULLER, Elizabeth 52
FULLER, Elkanah 70
FULLER, John 67
FULLER, Judeah 70
FULLER, Mehitabel 52
FULLER, Priscilla 44
FULLER, Samuel 70
FULLSOMAR, Israel 69
GAGER, Elizabeth 25
GAGER, William 21
GAIL, Richard, 94
GAIL, Sarah 94
GALLUP, Benjamin 42
GALLUP, John 62
GALLUP, Joseph 42
GALLUP, Nathaniel 62 108
GALLUP, Samuel 62
GALLUP, Thomas 54 62 104 108
GAYLE, Richard 32
GIFFORD, Martha 62
GILLET, Samll 61
GILLIT, John 1 87
GLEGHUNS?, Amasa 90
GLOVER, Henry 21
GLOVER, Susannah 45
GODFREY, Martha 37
GOODWIN, Nathll 51
GOULD, Thomas 46
GOVE, Nathaniel 1 58
GRAY, Ebenezer 43
GREEN, Ebenezer 39 100
GREEN, Henry 34 53 61 100
GREEN, Joseph 64
GRIFFEN, Benjamin 105
GRIFFEN, Joseph 105
GRIFFEN, Margaret 105
GRIFFIN, Benjamin 65
GRIFFIN, Joseph 55
GRIFFIN, Joseph 65
GRIFFIN, Margaret 65
GRIFFIN, Mary 65
GRIFFIN, Samuel 65
GRIFFIN, Sarah 65
GRIFON see GRIFFEN
GRIGGS, Patience 60
GROSVENOR, Amos 48
GROSVENOR, Ann 52
GROSVENOR, Caleb 52
GROSVENOR, Caleb 66
GROSVENOR, Ebenezer 48 52 66 103
GROSVENOR, Elizabeth 48
GROSVENOR, John 52
GROSVENOR, Joshua 48
GROSVENOR, Leicester 11 21 40 48 52 65 66 98
GROSVENOR, Susannah 52
GROSVENOR, Thomas 48 102

Windham (Conn.) Probate Records, Vol 1 (1719-1734)

GROSVENOR, William 48
GROVER, Jonathan 71
GROVER, Timothy 71
GULLIVER, Capt 45
GULLIVER, dau 45
GULLIVER, Jerusha 45
GULLIVER, Jonathan 45
GULLIVER, Theodea 45
GURLEY, Samll 63
HALL, Barnabus 87
HALL, Gershom 41 49 100
HALL, Isaac 100
HALL, John 10
HALL, John 5 810 20 25 26 27 74 77 78 83 86 87
HALL, Samuel 10 25 27 86
HALL, Sarah 36
HALL, Sheber 43
HALL, Stephen 10 26 27 86
HALL, Theophilus 63
HALLOWELL, John 15
HALLWELL, John 91 102
HALLWELL, Mary 46
HALLWELL, Mehitabel 91 102
HAMBLETT see HAMLETT
HAMLETT see HAMLETT
HAMLETT, Joseph 55 68 69

HAMLETT, Rebecca 68 69 79
HAMLETT, William 11 55 58 67 68 69 79
HANCOCK, John 56
HARRIS, Christabell 62
HARRIS, Ebenezer 13
HARRIS, Ebenezer 2 7 30 35 97
HARRIS, Elizabeth 7 76 92
HARRIS, Hannah 92
HARRIS, Joseph 92
HARRIS, Marcy 92
HARRIS, Martha 93
HARRIS, Mary 92
HARRIS, Peter 76 92
HARRIS, Rachel 13
HARRIS, Samuel 7 76 92
HARRIS, Stephen 92
HARRIS, Sylvanus 33
HARRIS, Thomas 92
HARTSHORN, Thomas 6
HASCALL, Samuel 45
HASKALL, John 53 100
HAYWARD, Elizabeth 45
HEBARD see also HIBBARD
HEBARD see also HOBART
HEBARD, Ebenezer 27 47 48 103 104
HEBARD, Joseph 36 103 104
HEBARD, Mary 36

Windham (Conn.) Probate Records, Vol 1 (1719-1734)

HEBARD, Nathan 104
HEBARD, Nathaniel 17 82
HEBARD, Robert 103
HEBARD, Sarah 82
HIBBARD see also HEBARD
HIBBARD see also HOBART
HIBBARD, Abigail 68
HIBBARD, Ebenezer 53 67 68
HIBBARD, John 56
HIBBARD, Joseph 6 53
HIBBARD, Martha 56
HIBBARD, Reuben 68
HIBBARD, Robert 53
HIBBARD, Shubael 67
HIDE see HYDE
HIDES see HYDE
HILL, dau 30
HILL, Isaac 5 16 74 75
HILL, Mary 37
HILL, Sarah 16
HILL, Solomon 37
HIX, Sarah 61
HO[LB]ARTON, William 50
HOBART see also HEBARD
HOBART see also HIBBARD
HOBART, Ann 16
HOBART, Deborah 16
HOBART, Ebenezer 16
HOBART, Elisha 16
HOBART, Gideon 16
HOBART, Jonathan 16
HOBART, Joseph 16
HOBART, Nathaniel 16
HOBART, Paul 16
HOBART, Robert 16
HOBART, Sarah 16
HOBART, Zebulon 16
HOLBROOK Ebenezer 58 79
HOLBROOK, Daniel 29
HOLBROOK, Ebenezer 52 55 67 69
HOLBROOK, Eleazer 55
HOLBROOK, Nathl 32 69
HOLDRIDGE, Samll 52
HOLKENS, James 31
HOLKINS, James 22
HOLMES, Jehosophat 48
HOLMES, Jehosophat 55
HOLT, Benjamin 17
HOLT, Daniel 9
HOLT, Paul 60 78
HOLT, Robert 70
HORD, Lydia 19
HORD, Thomas 19
HORSMER, Elizabeth 77
HOUSE, Dorcas 37
HOUSE, Lydia 37
HOVEY, Edmond 78
HOVEY, John 62
HOVEY, Joseph 58
HOW see also HOWE
HOW, James 64 65 107

Windham (Conn.) Probate Records, Vol 1 (1719-1734)

HOW, John 3 4 8 14 17 22 64 65 70 78 79 81 82 90 96 104 107
HOW, Jonas 64 107
HOW, Josiah 64 70 107
HOW, Lucy 64 107
HOW, Mary 6 8 22 91 95
HOW, Phebe 107
HOW, Phebe 70
HOW, Phoebe 64 90 96
HOW, Samson 78
HOW, Samuel 8 9 22 64 79 96 104 107
HOWE see also HOW
HOWE, John 15 31
HOWE, Josiah 31
HOWE, Mary 31
HOWE, Sampson 46
HOWE, Samuel 31 78
HUBBARD, Mr 61
HUBBARD, Sarah 104
HUCHISON, John 79
HUCHISON, Samuel 4 76
HULE, Sarah 7
HULIT, Daniel 59
HUNT, Ebenezer 18
HUNT, Elizabeth 62
HUNT, Hannah 18
HUNT, Thomas 37 110
HUNTINGTON, Caleb 26
HUNTINGTON, Christopher 76
HUNTINGTON, Daniel 58
HUNTINGTON, Eleazer 62
HUNTINGTON, Elizabeth 14 16 52 76
HUNTINGTON, Jabez 85
HUNTINGTON, Jedediah 62
HUNTINGTON, Jonathan 6 16 47 52 53 57 63
HUNTINGTON, Joseph 53
HUNTINGTON, Lydia 16 62
HUNTINGTON, Martin? 81
HUNTINGTON, Matthew 16 102
HUNTINGTON, Samuel 76
HUNTINGTON, Simon 62
HUNTINGTON, Thankful 59
HUNTINGTON, Thomas 107
HUNTINGTON, Thomas 26 58 59 60 62
HUNTINGTON, William 62
HUTCHASON see HUTCHISON
HUTCHISON, Hannah 1
HUTCHISON, Hepsobeth 90
HUTCHISON, Hezekiah 1
HUTCHISON, John 1 13 20 32 33 71 90
HUTCHISON, Jonathan 1
HUTCHISON, Joseph 1

125

Windham (Conn.) Probate Records, Vol 1 (1719-1734)

HUTCHISON, Moses 1
HUTCHISON, Samuel 90
HYDE, Abigail 20
HYDE, Caleb 23
HYDE, Daniel 23 54
HYDE, James 20 107
HYDE, James 84
HYDE, Jonathan 20 21 84
HYDE, Mary 107
HYDE, Samuel Jr 23
JACOBS, Joseph 56 106
JACOBS, Joseph Jr 38
JACOBS, Mary 38 41 99
JENNINGS, Ebenezer 108
JENNINGS, Jonathan 108
JEWEL see also JUOL
JEWEL, David 51
JEWEL, Joshua 51
JEWEL, Nathaniel 51 53
JEWEL, Sarah 51 53
JOHNSON, Experience 60
JOHNSON, Jacob 24
JOHNSON, John 7
JOHNSON, Joseph 30
JOHNSON, Mary 24
JOHNSON, Nathaniel 11 21
JOHNSON, Smith 5
JONES, Caleb 72
JONES, Joseph 34
JONSON, Jacob 84
JONSON, James 84
JONSON, Mary 84 104
JORDAN, Elizabeth 30 32 89
JORDAN, Miles 30 32 89
JOYCE, Hosea 37 38 98
JOYCE, Samuel 37
JOYCE, Thomas 37
JUELL see also JEWELL
JUELL, Abigail 51
JUELL, Hannah 51
JUELL, Mary 51
JUELL, Nathaniel 16 48 103 104
JUELL, Sarah 51 103
JUOL see JUELL
JURDON see JORDAN
KENDALL, Deac 54
KENDALL, Isaac 4 49 52 63 72 105
KENDALL, Joshua 4 72
KENDALL, Samuel 5
KENNEDY see CANADA
KIBBE, Joshua 2
KIDDER, Elizabeth 43
KIDDER, Ephraim 43
KIDDER, Hannah 43
KIDDER, James 43 100
KIDDER, John 43
KIDDER, Joseph 43
KIDDER, Mary 43
KIDDER, Nathaniel 43
KIDDER, Sarah 43
KING, John 100
KINGLSEY, John 66
KINGSBURY, Bartholomew 2
KINGSBURY, Ephraim 3 8 15 23 30 31 33 35 37 39

Windham (Conn.) Probate Records, Vol 1 (1719-1734)

40 45 53 64 81 84 94 95 96 97 107
KINGSBURY, Nathaniel 8 9 14 78 81
KINGSBURY, Samuel 2
KINGSBURY, Sarah 2 71
KINGSBURY, Thomas 2 71
KINGSLY, Amos 61
KINGSLY, Elizabeth 61 66
KINGSLY, Ezra 61
KINGSLY, John 61
KINGSLY, Josiah 61
KINGSLY, Lydia 61 66
KIRTLAND, Daniel 42
LADD, Jonathan 29
LAMB, Daniel 47
LAMB, Jacob 47
LAMB, Jerusha 47
LAMB, Zerviah 47
LARANCE see LAWRENCE
LASEL, Joshua 70
LASELL, John 33
LASELL, John 94
LASELL, Joshua 48
LASELL, Joshua 94
LATHROP, Simon 58
LAUGHTON, John 56
LAWRENCE, Daniel 8 19 23 27 30 31 34 46 37 39 53 59 64 78 84 86
LAWRENCE, David 51 107
LAWRENCE, Elizabeth 36 97
LAWRENCE, John 50
LAWRENCE, Joseph 23 30 51 53 54 66 82 104 110
LAZELL, John 6
LAZELL, Joshua 19
LEACH see also LEECH
LEACH, James 84 110
LEACH, Joseph 110
LEACH, Mary 59 84
LEE, Elizabeth 87
LEE, John 90
LEE, Mary 90
LEE, Samuel 34 87 90
LEE, Stephen 26 27 87
LEECH see also LEACH
LEECH, James 22 23
LEECH, MARY 22
LEVENGS, James 80
LEVENGS, Joseph 66
LEVENS, James 13 34 39 57
LEVINGS, Benjamin 66 68
LEVINGS, James 66
LEVINGS, Joseph 68
LEVINS, Benjamin 7 77
LEVINS, Elizabeth 8 77
LEVINS, James 77
LEVINS, Joseph 77
LEWIS, Edward 60
LILE see LILLIE
LILLIE, Bethia 21 49 71 73

Windham (Conn.) Probate Records, Vol 1 (1719-1734)

LILLIE, Elisha 21 49 73
LILLIE, Elizabeth 21 49 73
LILLIE, George 1 21 49 71 73
LILLIE, Jacob 21 47 49 71 73 101
LILLIE, Lidia 21 49 73
LILLIE, Mary 21 49
LILLIE, Reuben 21 49 73
LILLIE, Sarah 21 73
LILLY see LILLIE
LIMOND see LYMAN
LINCOLN, Ruth 62
LOOMIS, __akiniah 77
LOOMIS, Caleb 73
LOOMIS, Ephraim 21
LOOMIS, Ezekiel 58
LOOMIS, Thomas 62
LOOMIS, Zachariah 57
LOTHROP, Thomas 34
LOVEJOY, Ann 35 40 95 100
LOVEJOY, Bathsheba 35 80
LOVEJOY, Bathua 95
LOVEJOY, Benjamin 35 95
LOVEJOY, Elizabeth 35 95
LOVEJOY, Freelove 35 95
LOVEJOY, John 14 35 69 80 95
LOVEJOY, Naomi 35 69 95
LOVEJOY, Richard 35 95
LOWERING, Mr 61
LUCE, Ann 28
LUCE, Benjamin 28 55
LUCE, Grace 28 53 89 104
LUCE, Israel 28 29 55 70 89
LUCE, Jonah 70
LUCE, Joseph 28 89 104
LUCE, Josiah 27 87
LUCE, Mary 28 70
LUCE, Mrs 53
LUCE, Nathaniel 70
LUCE, Sarah 87
LUCE, Thankful 28 70
LUMES see LOOMIS
LUMMAS see LOOMIS
LYMAN, Ebenezer 58
LYMAN, Isaac 69
LYMAN, Jonathan 79
LYMAN, Josiah 4 74
LYMAN, Rebecca 69
LYON, Abial, 79
MACKDOWELL see MCDOWELL
MANNING, Abigail 42 99
MANNING, David 42 99
MANNING, Hezekiah 42 99
MANNING, John 53
MANNING, Josiah 42 99
MANNING, Samuel 29 42 89 99
MANNING, Sarah 42 99
MARKAIN, Joseph 21

Windham (Conn.) Probate Records, Vol 1 (1719-1734)

MARSH, Eunice 2
MARSH, James 31 46
MARSH, Joseph 4 76
MARSH, Sarah 30 37
MARSH, Thomas 3 8 9 56 59 60 78
MARSH, William 17 28 31 39 61 95 96
MARTIN, Ebenezer 56
MARTIN, George 56
MARTIN, Jerusha 56
MARTON, Joseph 44 84
MASON, Abigail 58
MASON, Daniel 58
MASON, Hannah 49 103
MASON, Hezekiah 26 69 88
MASON, Jeremiah 23
MASON, John 69
MASON, Jonathan 69
MASON, Robert 49 52 69 103
MAYHEW, Benjamin 10
MAYHEW, Hannah 10
MCDOWELL, Angus 59
MCDOWELL, Archibald 54 59 61 67 101
MCDOWELL, William 54 59 101
MCMAINES, Daniel 31
MERIAM, Sarah 16
MESSENGER, Mary 58
METCALF, Jonathan 72 77
MILLER, Daniel 95
MILLER, Eliek Sander 95
MILLER, James 91 95
MILLER, Joan 95
MILLER, Margaret Hannah 95
MILLER, Mary 50
MILLER, Peter 91 95
MILLER, Robert 31 91 95
MINOR, Manassah 58
MITCHELL, Abraham 26 44
MOLTON, Robert 5
MONROE see also MUNROO
MONROE, William 56
MOORE see also MORE
MOORE, Dorothy 58
MOORE, Elizabeth 44
MOORE, Experience 44
MOORE, Joshua 44
MOORE, Martha 44
MOORE, Tamerson 44
MOORE, William 100
MOORE, William 44
MORE see also MOORE
MORE, Joshua 41 58
MORE, Tamerson 41
MORE, William 41
MOREHOUSE, Peter 58
MOREY, John 84
MORGAN, Abigail 10
MORGAN, Isaac 10
MORY, Ephraim 21
MORY, John 21
MORY, Linsford 21

Windham (Conn.) Probate Records, Vol 1 (1719-1734)

MORY, Margaret 21
MUDG, Charles 58
MUNROO see also MONROE
MUNROO, David 22
MUNROO, Deborah 96
MURDOCK, Samuel 23
NANPOLT?, Timothy 87
NATAHANK, Margaret 45
NEFF, Clement 22 23 84
NEWCOMB, John 37
NEWCOMB, John 90
NEWCOMB, Simon 23 35 72
NEWCOMBE, John 32
NEWCOMBE, Judith 44
NEWCOMBE, Simon 2 72
NILES, dau 45
NILES, Elizabeth 45
NILES, Mary 45
NILES, Nathaniel 45
NILES, Samuel 45
NILES, Sarah 45
NOTT, Nathaniel 47
OATS, Dorothy 37
ORNE, Simon, 7 76
OTIS, James 110
OWEN, Margaret 44
OWEN, Ruth 44
OXENBRIDGE, Martha 45
PAINE, Constance 16
PAINE, Elisha 1 12 16 83
PAINE, Margaret 45

PAINE, Samuel 63 108
PAINE, Sarah 42 94
PAINE, Seth 52 108
PAINE, Solomon 41 42 92 94 95
PAINE, William 93
PALMAR see PALMER
PALMER, Benjamin 16 30 82
PALMER, Deborah 51
PALMER, Elihu 51
PALMER, Gershom 51 61
PALMER, Jonah 17 47 48 51 52 75 103
PALMER, Jonah 32 103
PALMER, Jonathan 51 55 105
PALMER, Mary 30
PALMER, Samuel 1 17 21 27 42 71 73 99
PALMER, Sarah 105
PALMER, Seth 63 75
PALMOUR see PALMER
PARHAM, Dorothy 20
PARHAM, Joseph 20
PARK, Elsabath 1 61
PARK, Isaac 1 30 61 89
PARK, Robert 30 42
PARK, William 89
PARKER, Frances 80
PARKER, Francis 13
PARKER, Isaac 12
PARKER, Jacob 60 72 108
PARKER, Martha 80
PARKER, Mary 37

Windham (Conn.) Probate Records, Vol 1 (1719-1734)

PARKER, Sarah 56
PARKER, Thankful 60
PARKHURST, Abigail 96
PARKHURST, Eunice 2 4
PARKHURST, Hannah 3 4
PARKHURST, John 2 4 22 35 40 72 77 80 92 95 96 104
PARKHURST, Jonathan 95
PARKHURST, Joseph 2 4 72 99
PARKHURST, Mary 3 4
PARKHURST, Samuel 2 3 4 72 80
PARKHURST, Timothy 2 3 4 8 9 72 80
PARKMAN, Elihu 53
PARKMAN, Samuel 72
PARMOUR?, Jonah 32
PARTRIDGE, George 23 33 85 94
PATRICK, Elizabeth 42
PATRICK, Matthew 42
PAYNE see PAINE
PAYSON, Elizabeth 50
PAYSON, Rev. 50
PERRY, John 54 60 104
PHELPS, Abigil 67
PHELPS, Ann 67
PHELPS, Benjamin 63 67 105
PHELPS, Jedediah 105
PHELPS, Joseph 23 29 35 105

PHELPS, Martha 67
PHILIPS, Nathaniel 107
PIERCE, Benjamin 58
PIERCE, Caleb 27 36 41 79 98
PIERCE, Elizabeth 25
PIERCE, Francis 55
PIERCE, Hannah 30 41 98
PIERCE, Jediah 26
PIERCE, Nathaniel 25
PIERCE, Phoebe 63
PIERCE, Timothy 5 14 62 63
PIKE, James 71
PIKE, John 1 49 71 92
PIKE, Jonathan 71
PIKE, Sarah 92
PIKE?, John 20
PIKE?, Sarah 20
PINNO, Dorothy 90
PINNO, James 37 90
PITTS, John 55
POLLET, Richard 42
POLLOT, Hezekiah 54
PORTER, Experience 63
PORTER, John 58
PORTER, Nathll 57
PORTER, Thankful 58
PORTER, Thomas 58 59 65 97 98 106
POWELL, Abigail 17
POWELL, Abigail 30
POWELL, Mary 36 41 98
POWELl, Phelix 30
POWELL, Rowland 41 98

Windham (Conn.) Probate Records, Vol 1 (1719-1734)

POWELL, Stephen 43
PRESTON, John 109
PRESTON, Joseph 70
PRESTON, Joshua 68
PRESTON, Levi 68
PRESTON, Samuel 68
PRICE, Grace 6
PRICE, Sarah 6 75
PRICE, William 5 7 75
PRINCE, Thomas 50
PROCTOR, Josiah 13 46
RAYNSFORD, Edward 32
READ, David 51
READ, Hannah 51
READ, John 51 98
READ, Jonathan 47 51
READ, Mehetable 51
READ, Ruth 51 53
READ, Solomon 51
REED, Nathaniel 33
RICE, Jonathan 20
RICE, Ruth 20
RICE, Samuel 55
RICHARDS, Nathaniel 103
RICHARDSON, James 14 81
RICHARDSON, Mary 81
RIGBE see RIGBY
RIGBY, Hannah 15 24 39 81 99
RIGBY, Jonathan 15 24 80 99
RIGBY, Susanna 15 99
RIGHT see WRIGHT

RIPLEY, Anne 10
RIPLEY, Hezekiah 99
RIPLEY, Jeremiah 20 25 36 51 86 88
RIPLEY, John 36
RIPLEY, Joshua 10
ROAS see ROSE
ROBBINS, Nathaniel 12 39 83
ROGERS, Anna 42
ROGERS, Daniel 50
ROGERS, Janet 42
ROGERS, John 42 50
ROGERS, Martha 50
ROGERS, Nathaniel 50
ROGERS, Rev. 50 51
ROGERS, Richard 50
ROGERS, Samll 50
ROGERS, William 42 46 101
ROICE see ROYCE
ROOD, John 36
ROOD, Mary 60
ROOD, Thomas 36
ROOT, Mindwell 10
ROOT, Thomas 1 44
ROSE, Thomas 25-27 86
ROYCE, Benjamin 57
ROYCE, David 99
ROYCE, Jonathan 13 79 99
ROYCE, Ruth 79
ROYDELL, John 51
ROYSE, Daniel 6
RUDD, Elizabeth 28

Windham (Conn.) Probate Records, Vol 1 (1719-1734)

RUDD, Nathaniel 27 75 87
RUGG, Abigail 56
RUGG, Elizabeth 56 105
RUGG, Hannah 56
RUGG, Jonathan 64
RUGG, Martha 56
RUGG, Thomas 56 63 64 105 106
RUSEL see RUSSELL
RUSILL see RUSSELL
RUSSELL, Benjamin 57
RUSSELL, John 80
RUSSELL, Mary 96
RUSSELL, William 81
SABIN, Eleazer 55
SABIN, Nehemiah 48 52
SALTONSTALL, Gurdon 50
SALTONSTALL, Mary 50 51 103
SALTONSTALL, Nathaniel 50
SALTONSTALL, Roswell 50
SCARBROUGH, Dorothy 68
SCARBROUGH, John 68
SCOTT, Benjamin 20 52 65 71 86 104
SCOTT, Ichabod 65
SCOTT, Mary 104
SCOTT, Peter 65 71
SCOTT, sister 45
SCOTT, Zebediah 71
SEABURY, Benjamin 85

SESSIONS, Elizabeth 59
SESSIONS, Nathaniel 11 110
SESTIONS see SESSIONS
SEWALL, Joseph 50
SHARP, William 55
SHAW, Joannah 5
SHAW, William 5 74
SHEPARD see also SHEPHARD
SHEPARD, Benjamin 23 104
SHEPARD, David 23 84 104
SHEPARD, Eleanor 23 78 83 84 104
SHEPARD, Isaac 25
SHEPARD, Jonas 25
SHEPARD, Jonathan 23 84 104
SHEPARD, Luce 24 104
SHEPARD, Nathan 23 84 104
SHEPARD, Samuel 8 23 78 83 84 104
SHEPHARD, Benjamin 54
SHEPHARD, David 54
SHEPHARD, Eleanor 54
SHEPHARD, Jonathan 54
SHEPHARD, Luce 54 65 84
SHEPHARD, Nathan 54 110
SHEPHARD, Samll 54 65 110

Windham (Conn.) Probate Records, Vol 1 (1719-1734)

SILSBY, Jonathan 21 28 49 71 73
SIMON, Jacob 5
SIMONS, David 20 86
SIMONS, Ebenezer 20 86
SIMONS, Jacob 20 32 82 85 86 93
SIMONS, Jonathan 20 32 85 93
SIMONS, Miriam 93
SIMONS, Robert 17 20 82 85
SIMONS, Tamson 85
SKIFF, Abigail 6
SKIFF, Hannah 6 75
SKIFF, Nathaniel 7 10 63 75
SKIFF, Ruth 7
SKIFF, Sarah 7
SLAPP, John 59
SMALLEY, Benjamin 4 73 74
SMALLEY, Frances 74
SMALLEY, James 74
SMALLEY, Joseph 74
SMALLEY, Rebeckah 73 74
SMITH, Elisha 70
SMITH, Francis 62
SMITH, Henry 38 40
SMITH, Jemima 19
SMITH, John 10 20 26 62 83 84 86
SMITH, Joseph 19
SMITH, Martha 70 85
SMITH, Moses 55
SMITH, Seth 7 77
SMITH, Seth 85
SMITH, Susannah 20 26 27 86
SMITH, Thomas 19
SNOW, Samuel 50 52
SOUTHARD, Elizabeth 44
SOUTHWORTH, Nathaniel 38
SPALDING see SPAULDING
SPAULDING, Benjamin 15
SPAULDING, Bridgit 83
SPAULDING, Dorothy 17 82
SPAULDING, Edward 10 16 17 25 38 64 81-84 107
SPAULDING, Elizabeth 20 27 86
SPAULDING, Ephraim 69 95
SPAULDING, Eward 20
SPAULDING, Hannah 19 29 99
SPAULDING, Isaac 2
SPAULDING, Jacob 19 29 46 80 82 99
SPAULDING, Jonas 24 83
SPAULDING, Jonathan 83
SPAULDING, Josiah 14 46 92
SPAULDING, Lt Samll 14
SPAULDING, Marcy 36

Windham (Conn.) Probate Records, Vol 1 (1719-1734)

SPAULDING, Mary 24 80 83 97
SPAULDING, Samuel 3 8 9 24 39 65 80 81 83 95 100 107
SPAULDING, Sarah 92
SPAULDING, Thomas 36
SPAULDING, Zachariah 24 83
SPENCER, Ebenezer 55
SPENCER, Elizabeth 51
SPENCER, John 29 42 51-53 55 99 103
SPRAGUE, Deborah 44
SPRAGUE, Ephraim 11-13 34 57 79 97
SPRAGUE, John 10 11 29 34 35 73 79 96
SPRAGUE, Lois 10 11 34 57 96
SPRAGUE, Mary 44 79
SPRAGUE, Samuel 12 79 97
STEDMAN, Experience 65 106
STEDMAN, Hannah 65
STEDMAN, John 57 65 106
STEDMAN, Robert 65
STEPHENS see also STEVENS
STEPHENS, Ruth 27
STEPHENS, Thomas 77
STERNS, Samuel 31 37 39 36 46 95 96

STETSON, Desiah 87
STETSON, Samuel 26 87
STEVENS see also STEPHENS
STEVENS, Andrew 78 86
STEVENS, Benjamin 78 86
STEVENS, Elizabeth 25 35 96 97
STEVENS, Fineas 78
STEVENS, John 22 35 39 86 92 95
STEVENS, Joshua 97
STEVENS, Josiah 47
STEVENS, Mary 25 27 35 78 86
STEVENS, Ruth 25 35 86
STEVENS, Samuel 78
STEVENS, Thomas 10 16 20 25 26 35 46 48 51 78 82-84 86 87
STEVENS, Thomas 109
STEVENS, unborn 35
STEVENS, Uriah 78 86
STEVENS, Zebulon 25 78 86
STEWART, Edward 99
STEWART, Elexand 58
STORRS, Elizabeth 38 41 96 99
STORRS, Hudgens 38 41 96 99
STORRS, John 38 41 93 96 99

135

Windham (Conn.) Probate Records, Vol 1 (1719-1734)

STORRS, Joseph 38 41 93 96 99
STORRS, Martha 38 41 93 96 99
STORRS, Mary 59 96
STORRS, Samuel 32 38 41 93 96 99
STORRS, Thomas 26 32 37 41 43 48 49 56 64 87 80 93 96 99 106
STRONG, Jedidiah 8 77 109
STRONG, John 61
STRONG, Joseph 58
STRONG, Noah 29
STRONG, Preserved 29
STRONG, Stephen 41 62 98 99
SULLARD, John 37
SULLIVAN, John 32
SUTTON, Seth 36
SWETLAND, Joseph 58
SWETLAND, Marcy 58
SWETLAND, Temperance 58
SWETLAND, William 58
TAYLOR, Mary 11
THATCHER, Oxenbridge 45
THATCHER, Peter 44 45 101
THATCHER, Ralph 45
THATCHER, Rhodolphus 71
THATCHER, Susannah 45 101
THATCHER, Thomas 45 71
THOMAS, Jonathan 45
THOMSON, Benoni, 66
THOMSON, Peter, 66
THROOP, Dan 22 85
THROOP, Dorothy 22
THROOP, Samuel 22 23 85
THROOP, William 23
TICKNOR, William 58 106
TIFFANY, Thomas Jr 60
TILDEN, Hannah 36 98
TILDEN, Joshua 36
TILDEN, Mary 36
TILDEN, Stephen 36 37 41 98
TISDALE, Abigail 29
TISDALE, Antipas 29
TISDALE, Ebenezer 28 29
TISDALE, James 28 89
TISDALE, Margaret 29
TISDALE, Mary 29
TISDALE, Mindwell 29
TISDALE, Phoebe 29
TISDALE, Solomon 29
TISDALE, Sybil 29
TISDALE, Thomas 56
TISDALE, William 29
TRACY, _____ 33
TRACY, Solomon 31-33 39 42 63 93 94

Windham (Conn.) Probate Records, Vol 1 (1719-1734)

TRACY, Stephen 57
TRUMBULL, Joseph 7 10 43
TUCKER, Ephraim 45
TUCKER, Joseph 48
TUTTLE, James 21
TUTTLE, Nathan 73
UPTON, Tabitha 6
WADSWORTH, Samuel 110
WALAR, Hannah 44
WALDIN, Dorcas 6 12
WALDIN, John 6 74
WALDIN, Joseph 6 87
WALDIN, Mary 6
WALDIN, Nathaniel 6
WALDIN, Sarah 6
WALES, Ebenezer 70 77
WALKER, David 55
WALKER, Edward 54 55 57 105
WALKER, Mary 54 105
WALLES, Ebenezer 85
WALLES, Estar 85
WARIN see WARREN
WARNER, Andrew 59 106
WARNER, Deborah 59
WARNER, Elisha 59
WARNER, Joseph 59
WARNER, Thomas 59
WARREN, Abigail 59 75
WARREN, Ephraim 13
WARREN, Jacob 2 8 9 14 15 17 23 33 37 53 59 63 66 74 75 84 89
WARREN, Joseph 3 37 90
WARREN, Sarah 89
WARRIN see WARREN
WASSET, Joseph 56
WATERS, Daniel 40
WATERS, Jacob 56
WATROUS, Isaac 65
WATROUS, Jacob 65
WATTLES, William 2
WAY, Mary 34
WEBB, Nathaniel 5
WEBB, Samuel 1 21 25 73 88
WEBSTER, Abigail 76
WEBSTER, Benajah 76 77
WEBSTER, Ebenezer 76 77
WEBSTER, George 4 8 73 76 77
WEBSTER, Jerusha 76 77
WEBSTER, John 8 77
WEBSTER, Jonathan 76
WEBSTER, Joseph 76 77
WEBSTER, Mary 76 77
WEBSTER, Noah 76 77
WEBSTER, Peletiah 76
WEBSTER, Samuel 76 77
WEBSTER, Sarah 73 76 77
WEBSTER, Zerviah 76 77
WELCH, Ebenezer 36 85 97
WELCH, James 23 25 35 85 97
WELCH, John 36 97

Windham (Conn.) Probate Records, Vol 1 (1719-1734)

WELCH, Marcy 36
WELCH, Martha 14 36 97
WELCH, Mary 97
WELCH, Samuel 36 97
WELCH, Samuel 97
WELCH, Thomas 36
WEST, Ebenezer 43 62
WEST, Francis 7
WEST, John 23
WHEELER, Benjamin 14 16 28 63 81
WHEELER, Edward 14 81 102
WHEELER, Ephraim 3 4 8 9 14 15 63 81 102
WHEELER, Isaac 22 28
WHEELER, Josiah 29
WHEELER, Mary 14 81
WHEELER, Olive 14 28 81
WHEELER, Sarah 96
WHEELER, Thomas 14 16 22 63 81
WHEELOCK, Ralph 4 6 73 75 96
WHITE, Abigail 38 110
WHITE, Elizabeth 33 93 94
WHITE, Joshua 70
WHITING Elisha 25
WHITING, Eliphalet 25 88
WHITING, Elisha 88
WHITING, Elizabeth 18 82 88
WHITING, John 25 78 83 88
WHITING, Joseph 25 88
WHITING, Mary 24 25 88
WHITING, Nathan 25 88
WHITING, Samuel 18 24 25 82 88
WHITING, Thomas 9 78 83
WHITING, William 24 25 88
WHITNEY, Anna 38 92 98
WHITNEY, David 51 53 84 103
WHITNEY, Ebenezer 38 40 92 98
WHITNEY, Enoch 40 98
WHITNEY, Ezekal 40 98
WHITNEY, Israel 40 98
WHITNEY, Joshua 5 12 23 24 30 82 84
WHITNEY, Mary 30
WHITNEY, Zachariah 40 98
WHITTINGHAM, Richard 50
WILCOX, Samll 47
WILEY, John 53
WILLARD, Hannah 50 51
WILLARD, Josiah 50
WILLES, Lydia 81
WILLES, Robert 81
WILLIAMS, 15
WILLIAMS, Bartholomew 46 97

Windham (Conn.) Probate Records, Vol 1 (1719-1734)

WILLIAMS, Catherine 97
WILLIAMS, Ebenezer 5 26 39 40 42 48 51 53 70
WILLIAMS, Elea___ 34
WILLIAMS, Eleazer 37 59 70 93 97 101
WILLIAMS, Elizabeth 5
WILLIAMS, Isaiah 5
WILLIAMS, John 52 61 63
WILLIAMS, Jos 26
WILLIAMS, Jos. 25
WILLIAMS, Joseph 5 8 16 17 25-27 34 54 78 86
WILLIAMS, Mark 69
WILLIAMS, Mr 42
WILLIAMS, Robert 46
WILLIAMS, Sarah 5
WILLIAMS, Thomas 2 5 19 35 74
WILLIS, Robert 14
WILSON, Dorothy 29 30
WILSON, Jacob 48
WILSON, John 29
WILSON, Joseph 4 72 80
WILSON, Mary 72
WITE see WHITE
WOOD, Mary 58
WOOD, Thomas 34
WOODWARD, Bethia 28
WOODWARD, Elizabeth 28
WOODWARD, Hannah 20 57 83 103
WOODWARD, Henry 4 13 74
WOODWARD, Israel 43
WOODWARD, John 2 20 24 27 28 43 44 56 73 80 83 88
WOODWARD, Joseph 20 28 57 83 88 89 103
WOODWARD, Nathaniel 8 9
WOODWARD, Richard 28 88
WOODWARD, Sarah 43
WOODWORTH, Amos 44
WOODWORTH, Benjamin 44 100
WOODWORTH, Ebenezer 44
WOODWORTH, Ezekiel 44
WOODWORTH, Ichabod 44
WOODWORTH, Rebeckah 74
WRIGHT, Abel 27 32 85
WRIGHT, Dorothy 103
WRIGHT, Ebenezer 85
WRIGHT, Ephram 85
WRIGHT, Hannah 39
WRIGHT, Jacob 5 74
WRIGHT, Jonathan 15
WRIGHT, Joshua 28
WRIGHT, Nathan 55 68 103
WRIGHT, Samll 44

www.ingramcontent.com/pod-product-compliance
Lightning Source LLC
Chambersburg PA
CBHW050643160426
43194CB00010B/1790